Muhammad

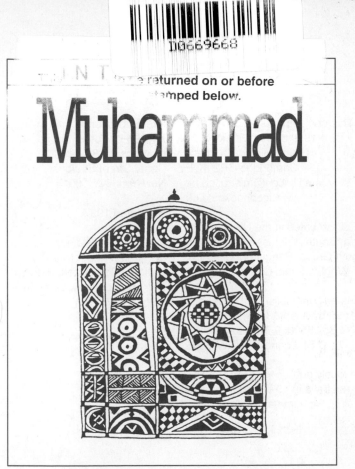

Ziauddin Sardar and Zafar Abbas Malik

Edited by Richard Appignanesi

Introducin Muhammad

ICON BOOKS UK   TOTEM BOOKS USA

This edition published in the UK in 1999 by Icon Books Ltd., Grange Road, Duxford, Cambridge CB2 4QF email: icon@mistral.co.uk www.iconbooks.co.uk

Distributed in the UK, Europe, Canada, South Africa and Asia by the Penguin Group: Penguin Books Ltd., 27 Wrights Lane, London W8 5TZ

This edition published in Australia in 1999 by Allen & Unwin Pty. Ltd., PO Box 8500, 9 Atchison Street, St. Leonards NSW 2065

Previously published in the UK and Australia in 1994 under the title *Muhammad for Beginners*

Reprinted 1995, 1996

First published in the United States in 1994 by Totem Books Inquiries to: PO Box 223, Canal Street Station, New York, NY 10013

Reprinted 1997

In the United States, distributed to the trade by National Book Network Inc., 4720 Boston Way, Lanham, Maryland 20706

Originating editor: Richard Appignanesi

Printed and bound in Australia
by McPherson's Printing Group, Victoria

As Salam alaykum: peace be upon you. I am Fez and, *insha Allah* (God willing), I will make sure that the authors keep to the straight path. Stay tuned.

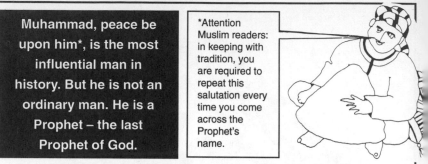

Muhammad, peace be upon him*, is the most influential man in history. But he is not an ordinary man. He is a Prophet – the last Prophet of God.

*Attention Muslim readers: in keeping with tradition, you are required to repeat this salutation every time you come across the Prophet's name.

Prophet Muhammad did not start a new religion. He conveyed the same message as all the other prophets of God - including Adam, Noah, Ibrahim, Moses and Jesus.

The eternal message that Muhammad preached is not named after him. It is called **Islam** which means peace and submission to God. The term Islam also signifies the natural inclination of human beings, a God-centred worldview, a civilization with over fourteen hundred years of history and an universalist world culture.

The followers of Muhammad are not called Muhammadan, this is an insulting term that first emerged during the crusades. Those who believe in the message of Muhammad and that he is the last Messenger of God are called **Muslims**.

'MOSLEMS' IS A CONDESCENDING COLONIAL TERM USED BY PEOPLE WITH STIFF UPPER LIPS WHO HAVE DIFFICULTY IN PRONOUNCING THE 'MU' SOUND.

The Life of Muhammad

 570 CE: Prophet Muhammad was born in Makkah (aka Mecca), in the Arabian peninsula now called Saudi Arabia. His father, Abdullah, had died a few weeks before his birth. His grandfather entrusted him to a foster-mother, Halima, who looked after him during his infant years. When he was six, his mother died. Two years later, his grandfather also died. The young Muhammad was now looked after by Abu Talib, his paternal uncle. Abu Talib was a generous but poor man. So Muhammad had to earn his livelihood from a tender age - he was thus unable to learn how to read or write.

Makkah was a desert city. Its main distinction was the **Ka'aba**, the house dedicated to the One God and built under divine inspiration by Prophet Abraham. The majority of Makkah's inhabitants were idol worshippers. Makkah functioned as a city-state, governed by a council of ten hereditary tribal chiefs with clear division of power. The most powerful of Makkan tribes was the Quraysh - the tribe of Muhammad. The city's inhabitants were poor but generous people, they loved poetry and war, and were fiercely loyal to their tribes and their gods. While it had no natural resources of its own, it was an active commercial centre. Foreign traders brought their goods to be sold in the local market. Muhammad became a trader and accompanied Abu Talib on business trips to Palestine and Syria.

> He is not one of us who proclaims the cause of nationalism and he is not one of us who fights the cause of nationalism and he is not one of us who dies in the cause of nationalism. Nationalism means helping your people in an unjust cause.
>
> Prophet Muhammad

WARNING! Islamic tradition forbids the portrayal of Prophet Muhammad or any of his Companions.

DECLARATION! "We agree and comply" – the authors.

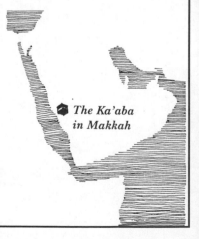

The Ka'aba in Makkah

The Pledge

One day, a trader from Yemen was cheated of his goods by a group of Makkans. When the trader asked for help, no one came to his support. So he wrote a satirical poem and recited it aloud for all to hear. When Zubair, one of Muhammad's uncles, heard the poem he felt great remorse. He called a meeting of city's elders and established an order of chivalry with the declared aim of protecting the oppressed of the city, local inhabitants or foreign visitors. Young Muhammad became an enthusiastic member of this organization which was called **Hilf al-fudul**. Later he would say: 'I am not prepared to give up the privilege (of being a member) even against a herd of camels; if somebody should appeal to me even today, by virtue of that pledge, I shall hurry to his help.'

Muhammad's Wisdom

M uhammad often helped the inhabitants of Makkah to settle their disputes. Once, the Ka'aba caught fire and was burnt to the ground. When it was rebuilt, all the tribes of Makkah took part in its construction. But when it came to fixing the sacred Black Stone in the wall, a quarrel arose amongst the Makkan leaders – all wanted to have the honour of fixing the stone. Finally, they agreed to select a judge from amongst them and abide by his ruling. The judge was Muhammad; and his solution to the problem saved the honour of all concerned. He spread a white sheet on the ground, placed the Black Stone in the middle, and asked the tribal leaders of Makkah to hold the sheet and carry the stone to its site. Muhammad than fixed the stone in its place. It was his integrity, honesty and wisdom that earned Muhammad the title of **Al Amin** – 'the trustworthy'.

FOUR TRIBAL LEADERS OF MAKKAH

Marriage

One day, when Muhammad was 25, his uncle Abu Talib said to him: 'I am, as you know, a man of scanty means, and truly the times are hard. Now there is a caravan of your own tribe about to start for Syria, and Khadijah, daughter of Khuwaylid, is in need of the services of men of our tribe to take care of her merchandise. If you offer yourself for the enterprise, she would readily accept it.' Muhammad replied: 'Be it as you say.'

Muhammad's courtesy, honesty and devotion to his work, earned the admiration of the widowed Khadija. So impressed was she with the young Muhammad that she proposed marriage. Muhammad accepted. At 40, she was 15 years older than him.

To bring about a just reconciliation between two contestants is charity, helping a person mount his animal or to load his baggage onto it is charity, a good word is charity, to remove obstacles in the street is charity, smiling upon the face of your brother is charity...sexual relations with your spouses is charity.

Prophet Muhammad

The Revelation

27 Ramadan, 611 CE: Muhammad was in the cave of Hira, a few miles from Makkah. It was his practice to retire to this cave regularly for prayer, meditation and reflection on the questions of creation, purpose of life and death, the struggle between good and evil. While in a state of inner reflection, Muhammad heard a commanding voice addressing him. Frightened, and with trembling voice, he asked: 'Who is it?' 'Read!' said the voice. 'I am not of those who read,' Muhammad replied. He was grabbed, hugged vehemently and then released. 'Read!' said the voice. 'I am not of those who read.' He was hugged again; and again for the third time. 'Read!' 'What shall I read?' 'Read! In the name of your Lord who creates, creates man from a clot! Read, for your Lord is most Generous, who teaches by means of pen, teaches man what he does not know.' He did. And Muhammad became the Messenger of God.

Muhammad returned to Khadija and told her what had happened. She covered him with blankets as he shivered with fear. 'O Khadija!', he asked, 'what is the matter with me?' In Khadija's mind there was no doubt what had happened on Mount Hira. He had experienced a revelation. And she became the first convert to Islam.

Muhammad first communicated his message to his intimate friends, and secretly, to the members of his own tribes. As his followers grew, he preached openly in the city and nearby communities. The Makkans did not care for someone who denounced their gods and ancestral beliefs. They launched a vigorous campaign to persecute the Prophet and his small band of followers. Makkans would force Muslims to lie on burning sand, place huge boulders on their chests, pour red-hot iron over them. Many early converts to Islam died under this torture - but none renounced their new faith. When the oppression became too great, the Prophet advised his followers to leave Makkah and go to Abyssinia. Many did.

The Makkans tried a change of tactic. Did Muhammad want wealth? Was he interested in becoming a chief? 'He can have anything he desires, if he recants and stops preaching.' Muhammad replied with his characteristic fortitude: 'By God, if they put the sun on my right hand and the moon on my left hand and ask me to give up my mission, I will not do it.' After several other attempts at compromise, the Makkans demanded that Abu Talib hand over his nephew to be killed. When the demand was not met, the city's chiefs decided to impose a complete boycott on Muhammad, his followers and his tribe. No one was to talk to them or have any dealings with them. The tribes living around Makkah also joined in the boycott.

Muhammad endured the persecution of the Makkans for 13 years. The hardship led to the death of his beloved Khadija and his uncle Abu Talib. He was constantly abused, sometimes stoned, thorns and rubbish were thrown over him - always, always he would pray, 'Guide them on the right path God, for they know not what they do.'

SCHEMING MAKKAN LEADERS

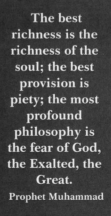

The best richness is the richness of the soul; the best provision is piety; the most profound philosophy is the fear of God, the Exalted, the Great.

Prophet Muhammad

The Night Journey

I t was during the most agonizing period of his mission in Makkah that Prophet Muhammad was granted a unique favour by God. He had a vision of an audience with God. The mystical 'Night Journey' – **isra** – took place from Makkah to Jerusalem, followed by the subsequent 'Ascension' – **miraj** – to heaven. Led by his celestial guide, Muhammad ascended, one by one, the seven Heavens of creation. At each Heaven he met earlier prophets of other nations – Moses, Jesus, Abraham and Adam, the first of the prophets. Beyond the seventh Heaven, Muhammad passed through the veils covering that which is hidden, until he reached the veil of Unity and looked upon that which the eyes cannot see, minds cannot imagine. It happened at the twinkle of an eye. And led to the institution of five daily prayers as an integral part of Islamic faith.

A solar eclipse occurred the day Muhammad's infant son, Ibrahim, died. Some Arab tribes were very impressed by the joint occurrence of the two events. Muhammad must be a true Prophet, they thought, if his loss was mourned by the heavenly bodies. Consequently, they flocked in front of his house and asked to be converted to Islam. The phenomenon, Muhammad told them, had nothing to do with the birth or the death of a mortal – it had no connection with the death of his son. Disappointed, the gathered tribes dispersed.

> No father gives his child
> anything better than
> good manners.
> **Prophet Muhammad**

The Hijra to Madina

622 CE: Exactly one year after his 'Night Journey', Muhammad was persuaded by a group of Muslims from Madina, a town 200 miles north of Makkah, to migrate to their city. As life in Makkah was intolerable, Muhammad agreed. Meanwhile, the Makkans had produced an elaborate plan to kill Muhammad. On the appointed day, the Makkans entered his house with the intention of stabbing him while he slept. To their astonishment, they discovered that Muhammad, accompanied by his companion Abu Bakr, had already left for Madina. In his bed lay Ali, his young cousin. The Makkans formed a posse and gave chase. Muhammad and Abu Bakr hid in a cave on Mount Thawr and eventually reached Madina safely.

The **hijra** – or the migration of the Prophet Muhammad from Makkah to Madina – marks the beginning of the (Muslim) calendar.

The Muslim calendar is a lunar calendar based solely upon the Moon's changes. The Muslim year takes no account of seasonal changes. In relation to the solar year, it recedes approximately eleven days each solar year, with the result that in each 32.5 years it passes through all the solar seasons. Thus, if in a given year the fasting month of Ramadan occurs during the heat of the summer, it will occur within the cool season 16.25 years later.

The people of Madina rejoiced at the arrival of Muhammad. The city also played host to hundreds of migrants from Makkah. Muhammad suggested that each working and well-off individual from Madina should take a migrant from Makkah as his brother. 'Fraternize in Allah', he announced, 'you are brothers.' As helpers, the folks from Medina were to share half their property and belongings with their migrant brothers from Makkah. The inhabitants of Madina accepted Muhammad's suggestion. But some people from Makkah did not wish to burden their brothers from Madina.

'SHOW US THE WAY TO THE MARKET,' THEY SAID, 'WE WILL MAINTAIN OURSELVES BY WORKING.'

Together with Arabs, Jews, Christians and others, Muhammad established a city-state in Madina. And with their agreement, he gave the city a written constitution - the first in the world. Apart from the city's governing structure, the constitution recognized liberty of religion, laid down principles of defence and foreign policy and organized a system of social insurance. Muhammad also made alliances and treaties with tribes living around Madina.

The Battle of Badr

 624 CE: The Makkans were not too pleased by Muhammad's safe departure and the establishment of the city-state of Madina under his leadership. They vowed to crush him. After thorough preparation lasting some two years, a Makkan force of a thousand fully armed warriors, many on horses, marched on Madina. Their objective was total annihilation of the small Muslim community of Madina. Muhammad decided to fight them outside the city, near the field of Badr. And so 313 ill-equipped Muslims, with two horses and 70 camels between them, met the Makkan brigade. The battle was fierce and swift. Seventy Makkans were killed; seventy were captured. The Makkans fled, leaving much of what they had brought behind them. A few days after the battle, Muhammad released the prisoners captured at Badr.

The Battle of Uhad

The humiliating defeat at Badr only increased the Makkans' resolve to crush the Muslim community of Madina. They returned a year later with three thousand well armed men. This time they were met by 700 Muslims at the base of Mount Uhad, just outside Madina. Once again, the battle was fierce and swift. The lines of the enemy were broken and they were repulsed. A group of Muslim archers on top of Mount Uhad, under strict orders not to move, sensed easy victory and abandoned their position. This enabled the Makkans to re-group and counter-attack. The resulting confusion turned certain victory to near defeat. Seventy Muslims died and Muhammad was wounded. But the enemy was held at the foot of the hill. So they called it a day and promised to return the following year.

Muhammad's instruction to his troops going in battle:
▶ Molest not the harmless inmates or those who are ill in bed.
▶ Abstain from demolishing the dwellings of the unresisting inhabitants.
▶ Destroy not the means of their subsistence, nor their fruit trees.
▶ And touch not the palm.

626 CE: The Makkans spent much of the year planning a mega-campaign against the Muslims. They combined forces with various Jewish tribes, as well as tribes of the north, south and east of Madina and gathered a mighty alliance of ten thousand strong against the Prophet.

Muhammad consulted his companions for advice on how to defend Madina. At the suggestion of Salman al-Farsi, a Persian Muslim, he decided to defend the city by digging a trench around it. The Muslims worked day and night for twenty days to surround the city with a huge trench.

The Makkan army tried for thirty days and thirty nights to cross the trench, but could not. 'By our gods,' swore the mighty Makkan force, this is a trick the Arabs never play.' And left without a battle.

The Treaty of Hudaybia

Muhammad eventually persuaded the Makkans to sign the famous treaty of Hudaybia.

Muhammad now devoted time to preaching his message outside Madina. He sent emissaries to the rulers of the neighbouring countries inviting them to the faith of Islam. Some of these rulers accepted Islam and suffered for their faith. The Byzantine priest, Dughatir, was lynched by a mob for embracing Islam. The prefect of Palestine was decapitated and crucified by order of the emperor. Many Muslim emissaries were killed.

Makkah Falls

January 630 CE: After repeated violations of the treaty, Muhammad gave the Makkans an ultimatum: to respect the treaty or declare the truce null and void. The Makkans chose the later option and thus woke up one morning to find an army of ten thousand Muslims marching on their city. They offered no resistance and the Muslims occupied the city without a battle.

The elders of the city stood, with their heads bowed, in front of Muhammad. What would Muhammad do to 'these' men - the very men who treated him so cruelly. To the likes of Hind who cut open the body of his uncle Hamzah and chewed his heart? 'What kind of treatment do you expect from me?' asked Muhammad of the gathered Makkans. They did not answer. So Muhammad answered for them. 'May God pardon you,' he announced. 'Go in peace. I say to you as Joseph said to his brothers. There shall be no responsibility on you today. You are free'.

The Farewell Sermon

 631 CE: On the tenth year after the Hijra, and after performing the pilgrimage to Makkah, Muhammad gave his 'Farewell Sermon' to 124,000 Muslims who had gathered in the valley of Arafat.

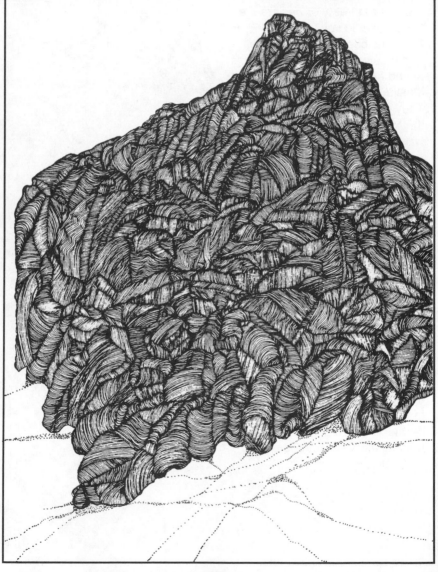

O people, lend me an attentive ear, *began Muhammad*. I know not whether, after this year, I shall ever be amongst you again.

O people, just as you regard this month, this day, this city as sacred, so regard the life and property of every Muslim as a sacred trust. Return the goods entrusted to you to their rightful owners.

Hurt no one so that no one may hurt you.

Do not take usury; this is forbidden to you.

Aid the poor and clothe them as you would clothe yourselves.

Remember! One day you will appear before Allah and answer for your deeds. So, beware! Do not stray from the path of righteousness after I am gone.

O people! No prophet or Apostle will come after me and no new faith will be born...It is true that you have certain rights with regard to your women, but they also have rights over you. Treat them well for they are your support.

Reflect on my words. I leave behind two things, the Qur'an and my example, and if you follow these guides you will not fail.

Listen to me in earnest. Worship God, say your prayers, fast during the months of Ramadan, and give your wealth in charity.

All the believers are brothers, all have the same rights and same responsibilities.

No one is allowed to take from another what he does not allow him of his own free will. None is higher than the other unless he is higher in virtue.

All those who listen to me shall pass on my words to others, and those to others again; and may the last ones understand my words better than those who listen to me directly.

Muhammad then turned his face towards the heavens and said:

'Be my witness, O Allah, that I have conveyed your message to your people.'

'My Lord, surely you have,' resounded the valley.

Death of the Prophet

a few months after his last sermon, Muhammad fell ill. He continued leading the prayers in the mosque in Madina until he felt too weak to stand. On Monday, the second day of the Islamic month of Rabi al-Awwal, and eleven years after the hijra (632), Muhammad whispered the words, 'Oh Allah, with the Compassionate on High,' and took his last breath. He was 63.

Outside the mosque in Madina, the gathering crowd could not believe that the Prophet had died. Then, Abu Bakr, his life-long companion emerged from Muhammad's apartment with tears in his eyes and calmly ascended the steps of the Prophet's Mosque.
'O people,' Abu Bakr addressed the crowd, 'verily, whosoever worshipped Muhammad know that Muhammad is dead. But whosoever worshipped Allah, know that Allah is alive.'

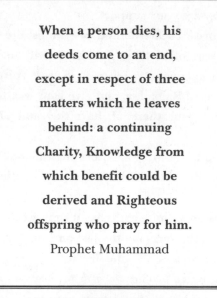

When a person dies, his deeds come to an end, except in respect of three matters which he leaves behind: a continuing Charity, Knowledge from which benefit could be derived and Righteous offspring who pray for him.

Prophet Muhammad

A Life of History

T he life of Muhammad is known as the **Sira** and was lived in the full light of history. Everything he did and said was recorded. Because he could not read and write himself, he was constantly served by a group of 45 scribes who wrote down his sayings, instructions and his activities. Muhammad himself insisted on documenting his important decisions. Nearly three hundred of his documents have come down to us, including political treaties, military enlistments, assignments of officials and state correspondence written on tanned leather. We thus know his life to the minutest details: how he spoke, sat, sleeped, dressed, walked; his behaviour as a husband, father, nephew; his attitudes towards women, children, animals; his business transactions and stance towards the poor and the oppressed; his engagement in camps and cantonments, his behaviour in battle; his exercise of political authority and stand on power; his personal habits, likes and dislikes – even his private dealings with his wives. Within a few decades of his death, accounts of the life of Muhammad were available to the Muslim community in written form. One of the earliest and the most famous biographies of Muhammad, written less than hundred years after his death, is **Sirat Rasul Allah** by ibn Ishaq.

30

The Hadith

The daily utterances and discourses of Muhammad, from the day he received the first revelation till his death, are known as the **hadith**. Hadith literally means 'statement': the hadith, then, are the sayings or traditions of the Prophet Muhammad.

During his life, the hadith were written down by Muhammad's scribes and companions on various media – papyrus, palm fibres, bone tablets, hides, white stones and parchment – as well as memorized. After his death, Muslims developed a special science concerned with the transmitting, validating and authenticating of hadith. This method of hadith criticism became a hallmark of Muslim civilization and generated a vast corpus of literature.

By the age of ten, Anas had learned to read and write. His parents asked Muhammad to appoint him as his personal scribe and attendant. Muhammad accepted; and the young Anas joined his band of scribes and accompanied Muhammad night and day. After the death of Muhammad, Anas became famous as a reporter of hadith. He used to unroll his sheets of documents and say: 'These are the sayings of the Prophet, which I have noted and then also read out to him to correct my mistakes.'

The Science of Hadith

ℭ he science of hadith collection, criticism and transmission involved

1. textual analysis
2. biographical analysis of narrators
3. examination of chronological accuracy
4. scrutiny of linguistic and geographical parameters
5. authentication of oral and written records.

Each saying was traced through a chain of authoritative transmitters, right to the lips of the Muhammad himself. The system of tracing narrators to the source was called **isnad** or 'backing'. The method of checking the quality of the transmitter came to be known as **ilm ar-Rijal** (Science of Biography). Thus a tradition of the Prophet always contains an 'isnad' which takes the form: 'so-and-so said that so-and-so said that so-and-so said that the Prophet said...'

A special group of scholars emerged who devoted their whole lives to checking each link in the chain.

▶ Are the individuals concerned reliable reporters?
▶ Is it chronologically and geographical feasible that the individuals in the chain actually met?
▶ Are the individuals of sound morals, not motivated by political or sectarian concern?
▶ Is the reported tradition logically and rationally consistent?
▶ Does it linguistically reflect the words of the Prophet?
▶ Does the reported tradition agree with the teachings of the Qur'an?
▶ And is it the kind of thing that it is reasonable for us to believe that the Prophet would have said?

Each tradition was analyzed on the basis of these and other questions and classified into categories ranging from authentic, agreeable, weak, narrated by a weak narrator, one with missing transmitter, downright fabricated and so on.

Using this elaborate system of categorization, early Muslim scholars sifted through literally millions of hadith. Imam Bukhari (d.870), the famous compiler of hadith, collected a reported six million hadith; but after criticism, accepted only 7,275 traditions as authentic. These are collected in his famous book, **Sahih Bukhari**. Imam Muslim (d.875) collected over three million; but rejected all except 9,200 which we find in his **Sahih Muslim**. There are six well known and widely used authentic collections of hadith, each known after its compiler. Apart from **Muslim** and **Bukhari**, they are: **Trimidhi**, **ibn Majah**, **Abu Dawud** and **An-Nisai**.

The Sunnah

ogether the Sira and the Hadith constitute the **Sunnah**. The word Sunnah means method, example, or path. The Sunnah, deeds and saying of Muhammad, the enactment of Muhammad's Divine Mission in the world, is an integral part of his message. As such, it is taken as a model of ideal behaviour by every Muslim. It is through the Sunnah that Muslims know and learn the ritual and spiritual aspects of their faith - how to pray, fast and perform the pilgrimage to Makkah. But the Sunnah is also the guide in moral and social matters. Thus a Muslim seeking a pious life simply follows the norms and patterns established by the life and traditions of the Prophet - the Sunnah is the way of Islamic life.

There are temporal and absolute parts of the Sunnah. Muslims are required to distinguish between these. For example, just because Muhammad wore a turban and rode a camel, does not mean that all Muslims must wear a turban or ride a camel. It is his insistence that the clothes that a person wears must be clean and must cover certain parts of the body, or that we must feed, water, rest and treat animals with kindness, that is the Sunnah to be followed. However, this is a contentious issue with some more tradition-orientated Muslim groups: they insist that all aspects of the sunnah must be followed in every detail.

> The Sunnah is a fundamental source of Islamic law. The Qur'an and Sunnah together are considered to be the theoretical and practical sides of Islam.

Some Sayings of Prophet Muhammad

❂ The world is green and beautiful and God has appointed you his steward over it.

❂ O mankind: God is One, your ancestor is one. You are all from the seed of Adam, Adam was from clay. The most honourable among you before God is the most God-fearing.

❂ The whole earth has been created as a place of worship, pure and clean.

❂ Little, but sufficient, is better than the abundant and the alluring.

❂ The value of the world in comparison to the Hereafter is like a droplet in the ocean.

❂ The superiority of a learned man over one who only worships is like the superiority of the moon when it is full, covering the stars. The learned are the heirs of the Prophets who do not leave a legacy of dirhams and dinars but only of knowledge.

❂ The search for knowledge is a sacred duty imposed upon every Muslim. Go in search of knowledge, even to China.

❂ God has not created anything better than reason, or anything more perfect or more beautiful than reason. The benefits which God gives are on its account; and understanding is by it, and God's wrath is caused by it, and by it are rewards and punishment.

❂ Poverty may sometimes lead to disbelief.

❂ God is gentle and loves gentleness in all things.

◎ **Hasten to do good before you are overtaken by perplexing adversity, corrupting prosperity, disabling disease, babbling dotage and sudden death.**

◎ Every religion has a special character and the characteristic of Islam is modesty.

◎ **Modesty and faith are joined closely together and if either of them is lost the other goes also.**

◎ Beware of envy for envy devours good works like the fire devours fuel.

◎ **God does not look upon your bodies and appearances, He looks upon your hearts and your deeds.**

◎ Beware of suspicion for suspicion is a great falsehood.

◎ **Do not search for faults in each other nor yearn after that which others possess, nor envy, nor entertain malice, or indifference; and be the servants of God.**

◎ Let the younger one salute the elderly, let the one who is walking salute the one sitting and let those who are small in number salute those who are large in number.

◎ **The most excellent jihad is that for the conquest of the self.**

◎ Were it not for fear of troubling my followers, I would order them to clean their teeth before every prayer.

◎ **A man should accompany his guest to the door of his house.**

◎ When you go to visit the sick, comfort them in their grief by saying, 'You will get well and live long.'

The Qur'an

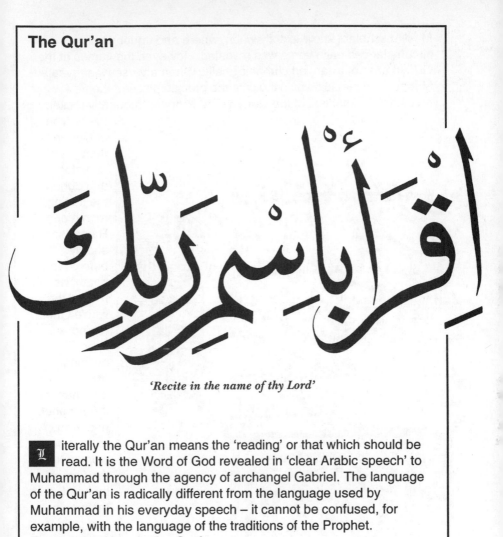

'Recite in the name of thy Lord'

L iterally the Qur'an means the 'reading' or that which should be read. It is the Word of God revealed in 'clear Arabic speech' to Muhammad through the agency of archangel Gabriel. The language of the Qur'an is radically different from the language used by Muhammad in his everyday speech – it cannot be confused, for example, with the language of the traditions of the Prophet. Essentially, **Islam is the Qur'an.**

Muhammad received the first Qur'anic revelation at the age of 40 in the year 610. The revelations continued to come for the next 23 years, in fragments and 'at intervals', ending 81/82 days before the death of Muhammad in 632, with the following verse: "Today have I perfected your religious law for you, and have bestowed upon you the full measure of My blessings, and willed that self-surrender unto Me (Islam) shall be your religion." (5:3)

Muslim scholars know exactly when, where and under what circumstances each verse was revealed. However, the verses of the Qur'an are not arranged chronologically. When a verse was revealed, Muhammad himself would indicate the precise place of the new revelation in total text of the Qur'an. The Prophet frequently recited the portions of Qur'an till then revealed; and during the fasting month of Ramadan, shortly before his death, he recited the whole Qur'an during special evening prayers. At the death of the Prophet, numerous men and women knew the Qur'an by heart; and the whole text also existed in written form.

✍ *The opening chapter of the Qur'an – from a Nigerian manuscript.*

The Authentic Qur'an

Efforts to compile a single, unified written text started immediately after the death of the Prophet. Abu Bakr, the first Caliph of Islam, instructed Zayd bin Thabit, the principle scribe of Muhammad, to collect all written fragments of the Qur'an. The complied text remained in the custody of Abu Bakr and, after his death in 634, was passed on to Umar, the second Caliph, who entrusted it to his daughter Hafsa (one of the wives of Muhammad). After the death of Umar in 644, Othman, the third Caliph, entrusted a commission, chaired by Zayd bin Thabit, to make six copies from Abu Bakr's master copy. When the task was completed – the copies painstakingly written down on parchment by hand – Othman gathered the companions of the Prophet and had a public reading of the 'authentic' edition. He then ordered the destruction of all other copies and sent the copies of the 'authentic' edition to different centres of the vast Muslim world. The text of the Qur'an used today is exactly the same as that of Othman's 'authentic' edition.

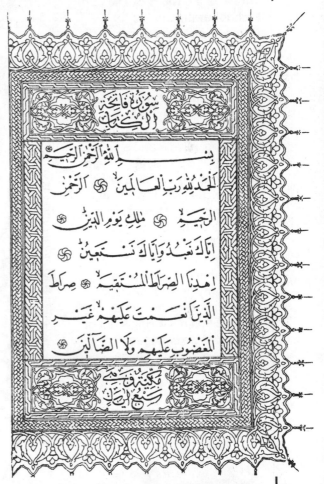

▲ *The opening chapter of the Qur'an – from an Indian manuscript.*

What is the Qur'an?

$\mathbb{T}$he Qur'an cannot be compared to other religious texts, for example the **Torah** or the **Bible** or **The Mahabharata** and the **Ramayana**, because it is not a book of narrative records of ancient peoples – although it does contain some stories of prophets and earlier nations. It is not a 'linear' text with a chronological order or a 'logical' beginning, middle and an end. It is rhythmic prose, epic poem and symphony all rolled into one sublime text. The whole text, containing 114 chapters or surahs, with a total of 6,236 verses, thus has a lattice structure which connects every word with every other word by rhythm, rhyme and meaning. The structure of the Qur'an ensures that not a single dot of its text can be changed, for even the minutest change simply throws the text out of sync.

"Allah is beautiful and loves beauty."

40

The Uniqueness of the Qur'an

I t is because of its special structure, the interlocking character of each word and verse, the eloquence and beauty of its language and the precision, economy and subtlety of its style, that the Qur'an is said to be 'inimitable'. It is not only physically impossible to change or corrupt it, but also beyond human capability to produce a single verse of similar literary merit as that of the Qur'an. The Qur'an itself challenges its readers to produce a single surah that could be deemed equal to any part of it: "And if you doubt any part of what We have bestowed from on high, step by step, upon our servant (Muhammad), then produce a surah of similar merit, and call upon any other than God to bear witness for you – if what you say is true! and if you cannot do it – and most certainly you cannot do it – then be conscious of the fire whose fuel is human beings and stones which awaits all who deny the truth." (2:23-24)

The special language and structure of the Qur'an makes it relatively easy to memorize. The language carries the reciter from word to word, the structure guides from verse to verse, propelled by imagery and picturesque style. The recitation of the Qur'an is a highly developed art form. It has two generally accepted techniques: a musically beautiful reading, **tajwid**; and a slow, deliberately simple chant, **tartil**. Young Muslims are taught recitation of the Qur'an from a tender age when they also memorize the entire text. The Qur'an is thus the only book in the history of mankind which is memorized from cover to cover. At any given time, there are literally millions of people who are **hafiz** – who know the Qur'an by heart.

Purposes of the Qur'an

T he Qur'an is addressed to all humanity without distinction of race, region or time. Its major themes are God, human beings, society, nature, reason, prophethood and revelation. The Qur'an speaks of the transcendence of God, the fact that He is beyond all perception of human beings - and hence beyond confines of gender, describes His attributes and contains the appropriate modes for praising Him. It describes the responsibility of persons as individuals and in society as the trustee of God on earth. The Qur'an makes frequent and repeated statements about nature in which the magnitude, stability and regularity of natural phenomena are stressed. Some 750 verses, almost one-eighth of the Qur'an, are devoted to extolling the virtues of reason. There are 250 legislative verses that provide the rules relating to social and economic life and penal and international law.

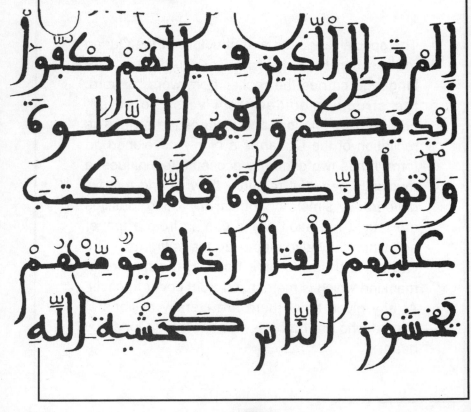

Essence of the Qur'an

T he content and message of the Qur'an is summed up by the Opening chapter, Surah al-Fatiha, which is known as the **Umm al-Kitab** or Mother of the Book. This short surah of seven verses forms the first part of every Muslim prayer and is repeated at least 17 times a day when Muslims say their obligatory five daily prayers.

The Opening.
In the name of God, the most Gracious, the Dispenser of Grace: All praise is due to God alone, the Sustainer of all the worlds, the Most Gracious, Lord of the Day of Judgement! Thee alone do we worship; and unto Thee alone we turn for aid. Guide us to the straight way - The way of those upon whom Thou hast bestowed Thy blessings, not of those who have been condemned (by Thee), nor of those who go astray. (1: 1-7)

(This is one of the most calligraphed chapter of the Qur'an – sample above, and on pages 38, 39, 45 and 46.)

Qur'anic Guidance

The Qur'an gives guidance by providing certain basic ethical principles and attitudes, fundamental values and norms, and by marking out sign posts which are known as **hudud** or limits of human behaviour. These general principles and guidelines are to be translated into actual practice by the intellectual and physical efforts of the believers. For example, the Qur'an tells Muslims to be modest in all aspects of their lives. It is for Muslim communities to discover what this general principle means in terms of dress or consumption. The Qur'an asks believers to avoid all forms of usury. Muslims thus have a responsibility to develop a usury free society. The Qur'an asked its readers to temper justice always with mercy. Muslim jurists have to translate this general instruction into a legal framework. Thus, general Qur'anic principles and injunctions are given practical shape by Muslims themselves according to their physical needs and abilities and constantly read and re-read, re-understood, interpreted and re-interpreted.

The Commentaries

𝕿 he need for interpreting the Qur'an arose immediately after the death of the Prophet. Early interpretations of the Qur'an relied on the comments and analysis of the Companions of Muhammad and their successors. Written commentaries of the Qur'an began to appear towards the end of the 9th century. Amongst the earliest and most frequently cited are those of **al-Tabari** (d. 923), **al-Wahid** (d.1076), **al-Zamakhshari** (d. 1144), **al-Razi** (d. 1209), **al-Qurtubi** (d. 1273), and **ibn Khathir** (d. 1373). These authors developed Qur'anic interpretation into an elaborate science, with numerous specialist branches, known as **tafsir**.

The opening chapter of the Qur'an with commentary in the margin.

Interpreting the Qur'an

All interpretations of the Qur'an have to follow certain basic rules. The most important source for the interpretation of the Qur'an is the Qur'an itself. When a Qur'anic term, phrase or verse is explained by another, no recourse to any other source is necessary. After the Qur'an, interpretation has to be sought within the framework of the life, sayings and actions (sunnah) of the Prophet – which provide a living commentary on the Qur'an. The rules and nature of the Arabic language are also a source of Qur'anic interpretation. Beyond these basic sources, the Qur'an has been interpretated in theological, literary, legal and rational terms. Muslim mystics seek the 'hidden' meanings of Qur'anic verses. Given that the Qur'an has many levels of meaning, the opinions and concerns of individual commentators also play an important part in its interpretation. As Islam spread among many different cultures, individual interpretations of the Qur'an gained a growing acceptance.

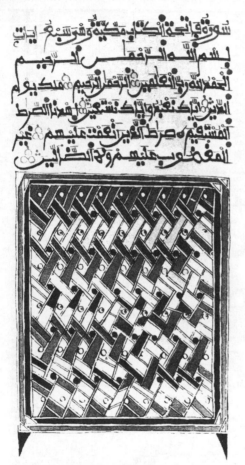

The opening chapter of the Qur'an calligraphed in Sudani style Maghribi script

Translations of the Qur'an

As the literal Word of God, the Qur'an is the Qur'an only in the original revealed text. A translation can never be the Qur'an, that inimitable symphony, 'the very sound of which moves men and women to tears.' A translation can only be an attempt to give the barest suggestion of the meaning of words contained in the Qur'an. This is why all Muslims, whatever their mother tongue, always recite the Qur'an in its original Arabic.

Throughout history, the Qur'an has been translated into every conceivable language. But translations of the Qur'an have frequently been used to subvert or cynically falsify its message. The Penguin translation of the Qur'an by N.J.Dawood is the latest in the long line of European translations which presents a distorted interpretation of the Qur'an.

Dawood: 'Idolatry is worse than carnage.'
Qur'anic meaning: oppression is worse than killing.

Dawood: 'The Hordes.'
Qur'anic meaning: The crowds.

Dawood: men to be 'wedded to chaste virgins.'
Qur'anic meaning: there for them shall be spouses purified.

It seems to me that the Qur'an is delibrately being given violent and sexual overtones.

Impact of the Qur'an

T he Qur'an has had an unparalleled impact on human history. It is undoubtedly the most read, recited, memorized, debated, analyzed and venerated book in the annals of history - not excluding the Bible. Listen to Muhammad Asad, one of the most respected translators and commentators of the Qur'an in the 20th century:

The Qur'an, "more than any other single phenomenon known to us, has fundamentally affected the religious, social and political history of the world. No other sacred scripture has ever had a similarly immediate impact upon the lives of the people who first heard its message and, through them and the generations that followed them, on the entire course of civilization. It shook Arabia, and made a nation out of its perennially warring tribes; within a few decades, it spread its world-view far beyond the confines of Arabia and produced the first ideological society known to man; through its insistence on consciousness and knowledge, it engendered among its followers a spirit of intellectual curiosity and independent inquiry, ultimately resulting in that splendid era of learning and scientific research which distinguished the world of Islam at the height of its cultural vigour; and the culture thus fostered by the Qur'an penetrated in countless ways and by-ways into the mind of medieval Europe and gave rise to that revival of Western culture which we call the Renaissance, and thus became in the course of time largely responsible for the birth of what is described as the 'age of science': the age in which we are now living."

Islam:
The Message of Muhammad
[the ideal version]

Those who accept the Qur'an as the Word of God and Muhammad as the prophet of God are called Muslims. A Muslim becomes a Muslim by declaring the **Shahaadah** - the formula of faith. The Shahaadah consist of two parts: one a negation, the other an affirmation.

The negation declares:
'There is no god except God'
the affirmation confirms:
'And Muhammad is His Messenger'.

"There is no god but God...

And Muhammad is the Messenger of God."

MUSLIMS HOLD THESE AS SELF-EVIDENT TRUTHS.

This simple declaration has profound consequences:

1. It implies that true existence is that of God alone; personkind and the entire creation exist only because God wills them to exist.

2. Since we exist by the will and grace of God, we are totally dependent on Him – our relationship to God is that between servant and Master.

3. As such, we are responsible for all our thoughts and actions before God to whom we will have to render an account of our worldly deeds on the Day of Judgement and Who will decide our final destination in the Hereafter, or the **Akhra**.

4. To prepare ourselves for the Final Judgement we must live a responsible and virtuous life according to the Will of God.

5. The Will of God can only be known through His Messengers; belief in God therefore requires belief in revelation – **the Books of God** – and **the Messengers of God**.

6. Of all the Messengers, sent to every tribe and nation, Muhammad is the Last, being the seal of prophethood and completing the process of revelation.

7. Since God is transcendent and beyond all human perception, He communicates His message to His Prophets through His functionaries – the angels.

Tawheed

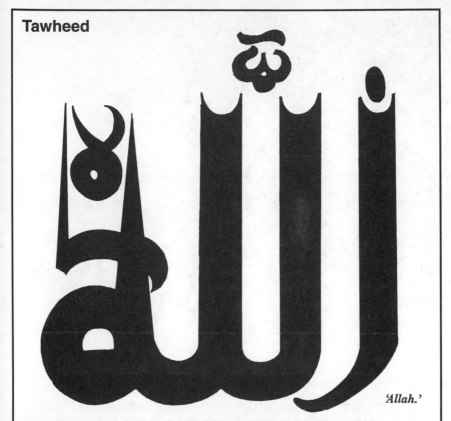

'Allah.'

T he declaration that **There is no god but Allah** is called **tawheed**. Tawheed represents the Islamic outlook on life, the universe and everything: it is the worldview of Muslims.

The unity of God is reflected in the unity of personkind. Since we are all created by God, we are all equal before Him. There is no difference between people of one race and another, between rich and poor, between the powerful and the powerless, between men and women. Islam is uncompromising on its stance on human equality. Moreover, since everything is owned by God, no one has an exclusive right to anything. All natural resources in the universe, land and capital belong to the whole of human race, and all its members have equal share and right of access to them. No person has a right to claim a bigger share, simply because he or she does not and cannot create or generate natural power independently.

Islam establishes a close and direct relationship between the Creator and His creation. In Islam no mediating power of any kind exists between the Creator and His creation: there are no churches, priests or sacraments. His absolute Unity is reflected in the unity of His creation in which each individual part is in harmonious order with the remainder.

A MOSQUE IS NOT A CHURCH.

The Pillars of Islam

From **tawheed** stem the 'four pillars' of Islam. Muslim spiritual and devotional life revolves around these pillars.

1. Salat or prayer, which has to be performed five times daily: before sunrise, between mid-day and afternoon, just before dawn. Prayer in Islam is actually an ensemble of inner and outer actions involving ablutions, intention of reciting the prayer, the request for grace and pardon, the recitation of appropriate phrases, recitation of verses of the Qur'an and bodily movements.

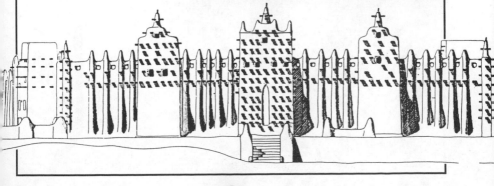

2. Sawm, or fasting during the lunar month of Ramadan, is a sublime spiritual exercise and a prescription for self-assurance and self-control. Physically, fasting involves abstaining from food, drink, smoking and sex; spiritually, it involves refraining from bad thoughts, actions and utterances.

3. Zakat, often translated as 'poor due' or 'charity', should not be mistaken for alms-giving out of one's generosity. It is a duty and a social obligation. Since everything one possesses belongs to God, the needy have a share in one's possessions and income and have a right to claim a portion of it. Normally an annual amount is prescribed out of one's income and savings as zakat.

4. Hajj, or pilgrimage, at least once in a lifetime, to the Sacred City of Makkah. The hajj involves suspending one's worldly activities, one's pride and ego, and surrendering one's whole being to God. The hajj is a physical demonstration of Muslim notions of human equality and unity – it is the personhood of Islam in action.

Every year, during the Islamic month of Dhul Hijjah, over two million Muslims from all over the world gather in Makkah for the annual pilgrimage. Hajj, which literally means effort, begins with the donning of two unsewn sheets of cloth (called the **ihram**), total abstention from desire and involves continuous prayer, chanting, inner reflection and movement: pilgrims move en masse from the Sacred Mosque in Makkah – the site of the **Ka'aba** – to the hills of **Muna** to the valley of **Arafat** to the site of **Muzdalifah** and return to Muna. It is at Arafat – where the two million offer a congregational prayer – that the pilgrims spend the supreme hours of their lives.

Khalifa

M uslim thought and action is regulated by a set of concepts and values derived from the Qur'an. After tawheed, the most important concept in Islam is **Khalifa**, or trusteeship.

Men and Women are khalifa or trustees of God on earth. This implies that the creation is a sacred trust from God and not the property of any individual, group or generation. It also implies that we are responsible for maintaining and preserving the integrity of God's creation – the earth, the environment, the flora and fauna. And we will be held accountable for our use or abuse of this trust both in this world and the Hereafter.

Adl

In Islam, **adl**, or justice, is a supreme value. Indeed, Muslim scholars have argued that the main purpose of revelation and the basic task of prophets is to establish justice on earth. All social life in Islam revolves around the idea of justice and believers are enjoined to behave towards each other in a just way. Justice begins with oneself and involves fulfilling the needs of one's body, mind and spirit. Family relations have to be based on justice: respect towards one's parents and elders, showing equal love and affection towards all one's children, and honesty and loyalty towards one's spouse are all manifestations of just family behaviour. At communal level, justice demands that one fulfil one's social obligations and responsibilities. It is a duty of a Muslim to stand up against all kinds of oppression, even if this involves one's own blood, society or country.

Ilm

T he establishment of justice in all spheres of human behaviour requires a certain degree of knowledge, **ilm**. Islam makes the pursuit of knowledge an obligation on every Muslim, male or female. A Muslim society can only be just when it is a knowledge-based society. Thus, the pursuit of knowledge is also a social obligation. Muslim communities everywhere have to ensure that experts in certain branches of knowledge – e.g. law, medicine, education, engineering - are adequately represented in the community. The Islamic term for an expert in a particular field is **alim**. It is significant that a religious scholar, a lawyer, a physicist, a sociologist, a philosopher – all are known as alims. In Islam, knowledge must be sought with modesty and humility, with the aim of promoting beauty and dignity, freedom and justice. Moreover, knowledge can only be sought by just means – the pursuit of noble ends by unjust means is not permitted.

Method of using the Instrument

Polar Star

Horizon

"Go in quest of knowledge even to China" – Prophet Muhammad.

The True Meaning of Jihad

onstant struggle for justice manifests itself as **jihad**. Jihad is one of the most abused and misused Islamic concepts. It means 'directed struggle' and can take a number of forms. A tradition of the Prophet declares that 'the supreme jihad is against oneself': that is, against one's ego, greed and insatiable desires. Jihad could also, for example, be aimed at the social development of a community. It can also be intellectual – directed against oppressive and totalitarian thought or towards the intellectual uplifting of a society. Lastly, jihad can also take the form of physical struggle against oppression and aggression. Jihad is thus much more than simply 'holy war'.

But jihad cannot be a war of aggression, or a war for territorial gain, or to impose a particular political order on a people. It is a defensive war which places certain responsibilities on those who are called to engage in it. As a moral exercise, jihad must be performed strictly under the Islamic rules of engagement. This means that innocent individuals, women, children and unarmed civilians cannot be harmed, property and environment cannot be destroyed, and places of worship of other faiths cannot be demolished. As such, kidnapping, hostage-taking, indiscriminate shooting of civilians, placing bombs in areas and buildings where people work, are evil deeds that Islam totally condemns.

Moreover, jihad cannot be declared by anybody on anybody. For example, jihad cannot be declared by one Muslim country on another, or an oppressive dictator cannot declare jihad on countries lined up against him. Jihad requires consensus of the whole Muslim community and a clear identification of the enemy as the aggressor or the oppressor of helpless victims.

Neither is a dictator like Saddam Hussain in a position to declare jihad on the Muslim and Western allies. Especially after his aggression against Kuwait.

ON THE BASIS OF THESE PRINCIPLES, TWO MUSLIM CANNOT DECLARE JIHAD ON EACH OTHER. THE IRAN-IRAQ WAR WAS NOT A JIHAD!

But the allied bombardment of Iraq and the suffering that it caused the Iraqi people is another story.
– And the Bosnian struggle against Serbian fascism is undoubtedly a jihad!

Shariah

hariah is normally translated as 'Islamic law'. It is, however, not 'law' but a set of regulations, principles and values from which legislation and law are drawn. While Shariah is eternal, Islamic law - like all law – evolves and grows and continues to change as the Muslim situation changes.

The basic sources of the Shariah are the Qur'an, the **Sunnah**, **ijma** or consensus of the Muslim community, and **qiyas** or analogical reasoning. Muslim jurists have also developed a number of supplementary sources for the Shariah of which **al-istislah** or public interest, and **al-urf** or custom and usage of a particular society, are the main.

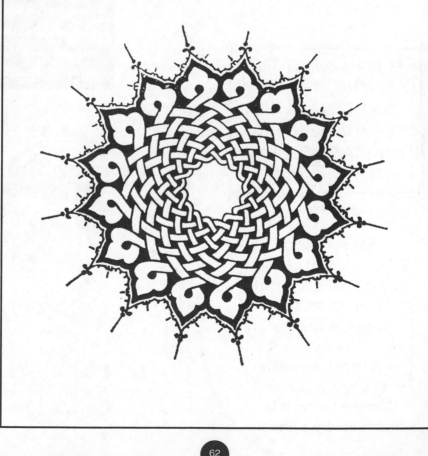

The Aims of Shariah

he ultimate aim of Shariah is to establish justice in society on the basis of compassion between human beings and between government and the public. It seeks this aim by emphasizing the rights and responsibilities towards each other of individuals and society, the community and the state, the rulers and the ruled. The main aim is the creation of a morally responsible society, with the accent on social, economic and political justice.

Shariah presupposes total freedom for human beings: freedom to act according to Shariah as well as freedom not to act according to Shariah. Those who wish to order their society according to the dictates of the shariah do so willingly and consciously.

Shariah also envisages a free society, a society capable of self-determination and in charge of its own resources. Unless a society has the freedom to harness and utilize its resources, it cannot distribute its resources appropriately and establish social and economic justice. The development of self-reliance, self-sufficiency and self-respect, both individually and collectively, are essential for a society that functions on the basis of Shariah.

Fiqh

Ɉ slamic jurisprudence was derived from the Shariah in the early years of Islam and is commonly known as **fiqh**. In its widest sense, fiqh covers all aspects of religious, political and civil life. In addition to laws relating to worship and other matters of religious observance, it includes family law, the law of inheritance, property and contractual law, criminal law and law relating to the administration of state and the conduct of war.

Literally, fiqh means 'intelligence' and 'knowledge'. Fiqh is thus what early Muslim jurists derived from the shariah with their own intelligence and knowledge – it is a human construction.

The Classical Schools of Fiqh

lassical jurists were unequivocal in declaring their rulings to be their own opinion which should not be accepted uncritically. They loathed the idea that a 'school of thought' should be formed around their juristic judgements.

But this is exactly what happened. Over time, a number of 'schools of thought' based on classical jurisprudence appeared. Five of these schools, each named after a classical jurist, are now predominant: the **Hanafi** school in the Indian subcontinent, West Africa and Egypt; the **Maliki** in North and West Africa; the **Shafi** in Malaysia and Indonesia; the **Hanbali** in Arabia; and **Jaferi** in Iran and Iraq.

Much of what goes under the rubric of 'Islamic law' is in fact classical fiqh: time-and-space-bound opinion and rulings – or **fatwas** – of early jurists. What this actually means is that Islamic law has been frozen in history and has remained ossified for almost eight hundred years.

I WOULD LIKE TO CHOOSE UM.....

Permanence and Change

The **Shariah** provides Islam with its permanent bedrock. But what is permanent in Islam is largely ethical: forms of worship, injunctions which forbid certain social evils, and principles which aim at promoting social, economic and political justice, and encouraging the pursuit of knowledge and reason. Everything else is subject to change. Islam envisages a dynamic, thriving and progressive society.

The principle of change in Islam is known as **ijtihad**. Ijtihad is defined as exerting oneself to the utmost degree to reach comprehension on a question of shariah. The exertion can take the form of new methods of reasoning, new social and intellectual insights, new ways of knowing and understanding. When the new understanding of the shariah acquired through ijtihad has the **ijma** or the consensus of the Muslim **ummah**, the global Muslim community, it becomes a part of Islamic law.

It is on the basis of **ijtihad** (all-around reasoning), **ijma** (consensus) **shura** (consultation) and **istislah** (public interest) that Muslim societies move forward, adjust to change, and Islamic law evolves and expands.

'There shall be no coercion in matters of faith'

W hile Islam is uncompromisingly God-centred and universalist, it does not see itself as sole repository of truth. Islam recognizes that all religions in their original teachings embody the same truth – and contain shades of truth even in their corrupt forms. Thus, Muslims respect the beliefs, teachings and institutions of other religions. Within a territory ruled by Muslims, all non-Muslims have the right to live according to their own rules and regulations and as equal citizens with all rights and responsibilities.

Both within and without, Islam abhors all kinds of monopoly – of truth, power, wealth, knowledge – and authoritarianism. Most of its general principles are designed to break down monopolies and subvert unquestioning authority. Islam itself cannot be forced on a society; and the Shariah cannot be introduced by authoritarian means. Even belief in Islam itself cannot go unqualified, for Islam does not appreciate blind, unquestioning faith.

THIS IS THE IDEAL VERSION OF ISLAM.

OF COURSE IT IS. BUT THE IDEAL ALSO HAPPENS TO BE THE TRUE ISLAM.

LET US SEE HOW ISLAM DEVELOPED IN HISTORY.

Formative History of Islam

The Prophet Muhammad left the decision of his temporal succession to his followers. After his death, a constitutional assembly unanimously elected Abu Bakr Siddiq, one of his closest companions, as ruler of Madina. Abu Bakr was a highly compassionate and kind leader. Examples of his honesty in matters of state are legion. He consolidated and managed the rapidly growing Muslim community with unparalleled ability.

Abu Bakr's speech after his election:

O people! I swear by God that I never coveted this rulership either by day or by night, nor had I any inclination towards it...You have placed a monumental task on my shoulders which is beyond my power to fulfil unless the Almighty comes to my aid. I have been made your ruler even though I am not the best among you. Help me if I am right; set me right, if I am wrong...The weak among you shall be strong with me until they have received their rights; the strong among you shall be weak with me till I have taken what is due from them...Obey me as long as I obey God and His Prophet. When I disobey Him or His Prophet, then do not obey me. ❦

Abu Bakr died two years after becoming Caliph. Before his death, and after consultation with other companions of Muhammad, he nominated Umar al-Khattab as his successor. The nomination was subject to the approval of the Muslim community which was readily granted. Umar was a highly skilled administrator, a clever political leader and military general. His selflessness and insistence in fulfilling the rights of the citizens are held in high regard. Umar ruled for ten years, from 634 to 644.

Umar's speech at his election:

O people! You have some rights on me which you can always claim. One of your rights is that if anyone of you comes to me with a claim, he should return only after his claim has been satisfactorily resolved. Another one of your rights is that you demand that I take nothing unjustly from the revenues of the state or the spoils of war. You can also demand that I increase your wages and salaries as more money comes into the public treasury; and that I fortify your frontier and do not put you in jeopardy. It is also your right, that if you have to go to war, I should not prevent you from returning home, and while you are away fighting I should look after your families like a father. ❦

The Seeds of Discord

Before his death, Umar established an electoral council of seven elders to decide on his successor. The Council selected Othman bin Affan and Ali bin Talib, cousin and son-in-law of Muhammad, and placed their recommendations before the Muslim community. The community was split. But eventually, Othman was elected as the third Caliph. Othman was renowned for his generosity, entrepreneurial abilities and gentleness. He ruled for twelve years and was murdered, as a result of open rebellion, in 656.

During Othman's reign a number of political groups had emerged. After his death, one of these groups campaigned for Ali, put pressure on him, and eventually succeeded in getting him elected as the fourth Caliph. Ali is admired for his bravery, humility and unworldliness. He was also a very literary person. His speeches, sermons, letters, administrative orders are regarded as models of literary expression, and many of his witty aphorisms and epigrams have been preserved. Ali was murdered in 661.

The Rightly Guided

The first four caliphs are known as 'the rightly guided' to distinguish them from the unelected monarchs who later established dynasties. Their lives and work are a source of inspiration. Their rule is looked upon for guidance in political and administrative behaviour.

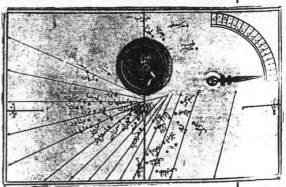

During the 30 years of the 'rightly guided caliphs', Islam spread to the four corners of the world. The speed and extent of this expansion is truly breathtaking.

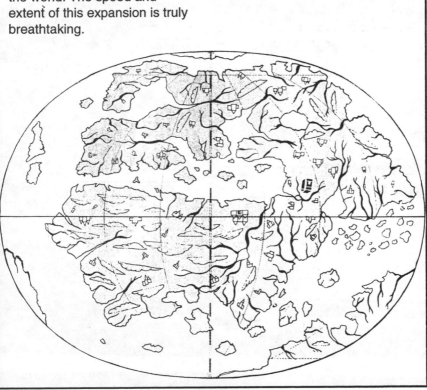

The Expansion of Islam

When Abu Bakr became Caliph, he discovered that the young Muslim state was being eyed as a juicy morsel by two rival superpowers: Byzantium and Iran. He organized an army and sent an ambassador to Constantinople in order to seek a peaceful solution. But Byzantium's emperor Heraclius had other ideas. So first Abu Bakr, than Umar, captured one city after another in Iraq and Syria. Wherever they went, the Muslim armies were welcomed as liberators and treated the vanquished with total respect, leniency and kindness.

Iran had a similar fate. When faced with Muslim armies, Emperor Yazdgrid sought the help of China, the King of Turkistan and other neighbouring monarchs. He was defeated along with his allies.

During the time of Umar, Muslims ruled from Libya to Afghanistan and from Armenia to Sind and Gujarat (in Pakistan and India). Othman's armies entered Spain as well as China. Half the then known world was under Muslim rule when Ali was Caliph.

The Rise of the Shia

T he murder of Othman and Ali had sowed seeds of dissension in the community. There were three competing groups: those who wished to retain the Caliphate in the Prophet's family, the majority who argued that the ruler should be elected on the basis of consultation and consensus, and a tiny minority who had the political ambition and military might to usurp authority.

The tragedy of Karbala is mourned annually by Muslims everywhere. It split the Muslim community into two groups: the Sunnis and the Shias.

The politically ambitious won. After Ali, Muawiyah, who had been governor of Syria for some twenty years, became Caliph and established the Umayyad dynasty. Muawiyah was succeeded by his son Yazid.

I AM THE FIRST KING IN ISLAM.

←MUAWIYAH

The successionists gathered around Ali's son, Husain, and rebelled against Yazid. Husain, his entire family, and his small group of followers, were all massacred by Yazid's army in the battle of Karbala in 680.

The Shia Concept of Imams

T he **Shias** differ from the majority Sunnis in their particular belief in **Imamah**. In Shia thought, true authority belongs only to the Prophet and his household. This authority, combining both temporal and spiritual dimensions in one leader, is manifested in the **Imams** (early descendents of the Prophet) in whom the religious life is marked by a sense of tragedy and martyrdom. Ali, the fourth caliph, was the first Imam; other Imams were his sons and grandsons. The Imams – who are **masum** or free from error and sin – are twelve in number; and the last Imam, the **Mahdi**, is said to be in 'occultation' or hiding and will reappear at some apocalyptic moment in the future. In the absence of the Imam, the religious and temporal authority is exercised by the clergy and religious scholars.

➠ Shiaism is a highly organized and structured religion – unlike sunnism which totally rejects the notions of an organized clergy.

➠ Shiaism also places greater emphasis on the hidden or esoteric meanings and interpretations of the Qur'an and the Prophet's life and personality.

The Muslim Civilization

T he essentially democratic and accountable character of the Islamic political order, introduced by the Pious Caliphs, changed when the Umayyad dynasty (661-750) established its power over the Muslim community. The Umayyads were neither all that pious nor devoted to the cause of justice. They were, however, good at building industry – and even better at conquest.

The 'Golden Age' of Muslim civilization begins with the rise of the Abbasids in 750. The five centuries of the Abbasid Caliphate saw the true flowering of Islamic genius. It also saw the political division of the Muslim community, first into two parts, and later into smaller and smaller kingdoms.

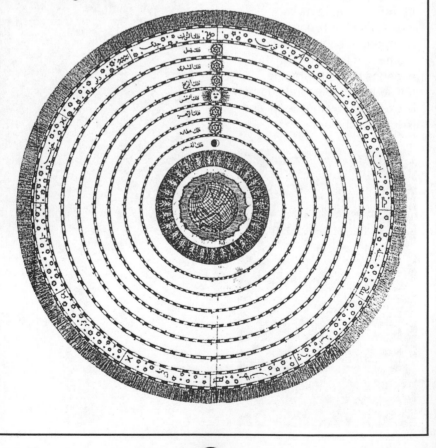

The Abbasids, who came from the family of Prophet's uncle al-Abbas, ruled from Baghdad. They had little interest in conquest but were passionate equally about learning and internal feuding. One feud led to the establishment of the Umayyad dynasty (756-1031) in Andalusia.

The Abbasid rule established an efficient, honest and vigorous administration. Concerned about the well-being of the population, the rulers took steps to ensure that their officials did not levy extortionate taxes, that the business class did not fleece the common man, and devoted great energy to building industry, commerce and institutions of thought and learning.

WHERE IS THE ZENITH?

The Knowledge Industry

Qur'anic emphasis on **ilm**, the pursuit of knowledge, became the main driving force of Muslim society. This urge 'to know' transformed Islam from its desert origins into a world civilization. At the zenith of the classical period, over 500 definitions of knowledge were competing for the attention of the believers.

THE ABBASIDS WERE ABLE TO TRANSFER THIS LOVE FOR LEARNING INTO A KNOWLEDGE INDUSTRY.

Initially, a great deal of emphasis was placed on translations and absorption of learning from other civilizations, including Egypt, Babylonia, Greece, India, China and Persia. Within a short period, books from Greek, Syriac, Sanskrit, Chinese and Persian were translated into Arabic - one of the most remarkable instances of cultural transmission in human history.

ACCORDING TO THIS...

After translation came the long and arduous task of critically sifting, analyzing and accepting or rejecting the learning of other civilizations. This is when the entire Muslim civilization became engulfed in intense debate – and the book became the key vehicle for communication of ideas.

At the beginning of the 8th century, books were made of parchment and papyrus which were difficult to handle and not easy to procure. The Muslims acquired the art of paper making from the Chinese, introduced a number of vital innovations and turned it into an industry. Thus books became accessible and relatively cheap. By the beginning of the 9th century, paper had become the standard medium for all written communication – and for wrapping groceries!

The Arabic word for a bundle of paper, **rismah**, has survived as ream in English.

A PERSIAN TRAVELLER, WRITING IN 1040, OBSERVED IN CAIRO: THE VENDORS OF VEGETABLES AND SPICES ARE FURNISHED WITH PAPER IN WHICH EVERYTHING THAT THEY SELL IS WRAPPED.

The Warraqeen

T he knowledge industry gave rise to the profession of **warraqeen** (lit. those who handle paper). The warraqeen were human photocopy machines: they copied manuscripts, accurately and rapidly. A book of a few hundred pages would be copied within hours; longer tomes took a few days. Most warraqeen made their own paper and managed their own bookshops – anything from a street stall to huge shops in pleasant upper chambers removed from the dust of the bazaar.

While **warraq** stalls were to be found all over such cities as Baghdad, Damascus, Cairo, Granada, Fez and Samarkand, the bookshops themselves were usually concentrated in a specific quarter of the city. Al-Yaqubi, the famous Muslim scholar of the late 9th century, counted more than one hundred bookshops in the Waddah suburb of Baghdad alone. The large and reputable bookshops attracted scholars from considerable distances and acted as informal clubs for academic discussions and meeting grounds for writers and thinkers with mutual interests.

Undoubtedly the most famous bookshop in Muslim history belongs to the tenth century bibliophile al-Nadim (d.990). Al-Nadim's bookshop in Baghdad was crammed with thousands of manuscripts and became well known as a meeting place for notable writers, thinkers and men of letters of his time. The annotated catalogue of the contents of his bookshop, **al-Fihrist al-Nadim**, is renowned as an encyclopedia of medieval Islamic culture.

The publication industry pioneered by the warraqeen worked on a system of mutual cooperation between writers and their publishers. A writer wishing to publish a book would announce his intentions publicly and would also contact one or two warraqeen. The book would be 'published' in a mosque or a noted bookshop where the author would dictate his book every day during an appointed time. Anyone could attend, and it was not uncommon for a large number of students and other scholars to be present at public dictations. The dictation would take considerable time, several months perhaps, during which the appointed warraqeen would always be present. When the book was finished, a handwritten manuscript was presented to the author for checking and corrections. Only when the author had given his final permission would the book be in the public domain and other copies freely made from the original. The authors, by agreement with the warraqeen, would receive a royalty.

The publication industry that dominated the length and breadth of the Muslim empire, from the 8th to the 15th centuries, was of mind-boggling complexity. At its peak, literally tens of thousands of books would be published in a single year. The oldest extant manuscript published in Arabic in this manner is dated 874.

The hand-written manuscripts were the size of the modern book, with writing on both sides of the paper, bound together by leather covers, and roughly twice as bulky as their contemporary printed counterpart. For example, the famous **Kitab al-Aghani** – a compendium of poetic and prose passages, with many stories about the caliphs, poets, singing girls and popular heroes – filled 5,000 leaves of hand-written manuscript; the modern printed edition fills five volumes, each of about 400 pages, and one shorter volume with 280 pages.

The demand for books led to the proliferation of private and public libraries. Book-lovers competed with each other in developing private collections and establishing mosque libraries. Public libraries varied in size from small rooms to giant complexes specially built for the purpose. The most famous public library was the **Dar al-Hikma** (the House of Wisdom) built by Mamun al-Rashid in Baghdad in 815. Its competitors in the city were the libraries at the **Nizamiyyah** (built 1065) and **Mistanriyah Colleges** (built 1227). There were equally magnificent libraries in all major Muslim cities, Damascus, Shiraz, Fez, Samarkand, Bukhara and Cordova. Cairo's **Khazain al-Qusu** housed over 1.6 million manuscripts in 40 purpose-built rooms. All big libraries had separate rooms for copiers, binders and librarians. All Muslim libraries were designed in such a way that the whole library was visible from one central point and followed an open shelf approach to storage and display. Nothing came between the books and their users.

At the time of the Mongol devastation of Baghdad in 1258, there were 36 public libraries in the city.

Institutions of Learning

I n the early days, the mosque served as the basic educational institution of the community. However, as the demand for learning grew, it became inconvenient to hold lectures and lively discussions in the mosque where so many people were trying to pray and memorize the Qur'an. Muslim educators thus developed a new type of institution: the **Madrassah** or the college. Among the first of these colleges was Nizamiyyah, built by Nizam al-Mulk in Baghdad in 1067.

In the Madrassah, the teacher (**Shaikh** or professor) would sit on a low chair, surrounded by students sitting in a circle. The honorary head of the college was a high official with a deputy or vice-chancellor to conduct the administration. Each professor had a number of teaching assistants and sometimes a special 'Reader' for reading aloud texts. There was no regular schedule and the students were free to continue their studies as long as both the student and the professor thought it wise to do so. Each professor started his course by giving an outline of what was to be covered, followed by a general explanation of the subject and the ways the authorities differed about it.

In parallel with the evolution of colleges emerged **jamia** or universities. The oldest university in the world is al-Azhar in Cairo, established in 970. The Qarawiyin University of Fez in Morocco was established soon afterwards. Apart from religious sciences, the university students learned logic, metaphysics,philosophy, mathematics, physics, astronomy, rhetoric and tool-making!

PROFESSIONAL CHAIR A MUSLIM INVENTION

The emergence of colleges and libraries raised a a fundamental question: How to classify knowledge for teaching purposes, as well as organizing books on a shelf?

Every Muslim scholar worth his salt attempted to produce a classification scheme. Al-Ghazzali's (d.1111) analysis of the social function of knowledge and its division into 'levels of obligatoriness' became decisive for the development of Muslim civilisation.

The classifications themselves led to the production of numerous genres of reference and bibliographical works: thesauri, dictionaries, encyclopedias, biographical, historical and centennial dictionaries, genealogical tables, geographical guides, as well as narrative and interpretive works of reference.

Arguments and Debates

I ntense debates, with fierce arguments stretching over centuries, were the hallmark of Muslim civilization. All variety of intellectual groups, with remarkably diverse positions, mushroomed everywhere. These groups had names like **People of the Tent** (who were Stoics) **The Brethren of Purity** (who were neo-Platonists), **People of Subjective Vision** (who were mystics), and **People of the Straight Way and the Community** (who were theological rationalists).

Of the intellectual engagements of this period, none was fiercer than the debate between the theologians and the philosophers.

"The Book of Debate" – one of the earliest printed books.

During the first two hundred years of Islam, philosophy stemmed from the Qur'an which provided rational grounds to demonstrate the existence of a creative, unique and incorporeal God. This rational philosophy was fashioned by the theologians and was known as **Kalam**. Kalam means speech or conversation and was based on the idea that truth can be found through a process of interrogation involving questions and answers.

The situation changed when Muslims mastered Greek philosophy. The champions of Greek philosophy broke away from rationalist theology and became known as the **Mutazilites** (Separatists). The reaction against Mutazilite philosophy produced a number of movements concerned solely with the rational demolition of Greek philosophy. But the major challenge came from the **Asharite** School founded by the theologian al-Ashari (d. 945).

RIGHT, WRONG,
RIGHT, WRONG,
RIGHT.

The Mutazilites argued that with reason alone one could know of God's nature and existence and what it is to act morally and immorally. Thus it was possible to perceive the truth without prophecy and revelation and men were free to do as they wished.

The Asharites argued that the comprehension of unique nature and characteristics of God were beyond human capability. And that, while man had free will, he had no power to create anything.

On both sides were some of the most brilliant minds of the time. On the Mutazilite side:

Al-Kindi (d. 866), known as 'the philosopher of the Arabs', encyclopedic scientist, author of some 270 books on mathematics, physics, music, medicine, pharmacy and geography, commentator on Aristotle.

Al-Farabi (d. 950), an authority on music, a mystic, master of Greek philosophy (and hence called 'the Second Teacher', Aristotle being the first) and author of **The Bezels of Philosophy** and **The Perfect State** (freely appropriated by St Thomas Aquinas).

Not to forget an assortment of Abbasid Caliphs, who saw themselves as philosopher-kings, and thought Greek philosophy a jolly good idea.

Ibn Sina (d.1037), child prodigy, encyclopedist, physician, psychologist, author of the standard text **Canons of Medicine**, master of, commentator on and corrector of, Aristotle: 'the most famous scientist of Islam and one of the most famous of all races, places and times' (George Sarton).

Ibn Rushd (d.1198), physician, scientist, linguist and 'The Commentator' on Aristotle and Plato: 'the greatest Muslim philosopher of the West'.

On the Asharite side:

Al-Ghazzali (d.1111), theologian, sceptic, believer, mystic, professor at Nizamiyyah college and the author of the monumental **The Revival of the Religious Sciences in Islam**.

Fakhr al-Din Razi (d.1209), mathematician, physicist, physician, philosopher, master of Kalam, author of an influential encyclopedia of science: 'one of the greatest masters in Islam'.

Ibn Khaldun (d.1406), historian, philosopher, pedagogue, founder of the philosophy of history and sociology.

When all the arguments had been debated and heard, al-Ghazzali's devastating attack 'The Incoherence of the Philosophers' gave the Asharites a clear victory. It was a victory based on superior arguments and rigorous logic. Ibn Rushd's comeback, 'The Incoherence of the Incoherence', one of the most powerful defences of rationalism ever produced, could not save the day for the Mutazilites.

In time, al-Ghazzali's ideas became the dominant mode of thought for the Muslim civilization.

AL-GHAZALI: 'THE PHILOSOPHERS ARE INCOHERENT.'

IBN RUSHD: 'TO SAY THAT PHILOSOPHERS ARE INCOHERENT IS ITSELF TO MAKE AN INCOHERENT STATEMENT.'

Sufism (Mysticism)

T he debate between philosophers and theologians tended to confine religion to dry rationality. It led many thinkers to seek refuge in the spiritual haven of mysticism. The early mystics used to travel freely wearing a woollen dress from which they took their name: the Sufis.

Sufism is based on the esoteric verses of the Qur'an and a number of traditions of the Prophet Muhammad. Its key concept is **tasawwuf** which is concerned with virtues like love, awe, patience, trust, fear, humility, quietism and practices like remembrance and contemplation of God, hunger and abstinence.

To acquire the ultimate experience of fana one has to follow a strict discipline by joining a **tariqa** or Sufi order.

❋ The Sufis believe that the ideal person is the mirror of God's attributes – and seek union with God by **fana** or by annihilation of the self and ego.↗↗↗↗↗↗↗

The first Sufi is said to be the great woman saint, Rabiah al-Basri (d. 801). She is the originator of the doctrine of 'disintrested love of God' which served both as a motive and a goal of her life.

The most celebrated experience of fana in Islamic history is that of the Persian mystic al-Hallaj (d. 922). Al-Hallaj became renowned during his lifetime for making mystical utterances in the streets. One day, in a state of mystical fana, he repeatedly uttered the famous words: 'I am the Truth.' After a number of long trials and counter-trials, al-Hallaj was finally executed.

The most talked about Sufi in Islamic history is ibn Arabi (d.1240). Ibn Arabi wrote deliberately impenetrable but highly influential mystical tomes and introduced the notion of the 'Unity of all Being' (**wahdat al-wajud**) to Sufism, a monotheistic version of pantheism, thus becoming the source of perpetual controversy.

I THOUGHT IBN ARABI WAS CRYSTAL CLEAR.

The Sufis have produced some of the finest poetry and prose in Islamic history. **The Mathnawi** of Jalaluddin Rumi (d.1273), which took 43 years to write, is considered a Persian masterpiece. Rumi founded the Sufi order known as the **Whirling Dervishes** . Other masterpieces of Sufi poetry include Farid al Din Attar's (d.1229) **The Conference of the Birds**, Firdawsi's (d.1020) **Shahanama** which contains 60,000 verses and Sadi Shahrazi's (d.1194) **Gulistan** (The Rose Garden) and **Bustan** (The Fruit Garden).

Literature

arrative literature evolved into a number of sophisticated genres. These included instructional narratives containing religious stories, glorious tales and moral stories and anecdotes. Popular romances were developed by storytellers with the accent on chivalry and tragedy such as the **Romance of Antarah bin Shadad**, **Romance of Bani Hilal** and **Story of Bakr and Taghlib**. Linguistic narratives, designed to show off language, played on the beauty and elegance of Arabic like al-Hariri's (d.1122) **The Assemblies**. And philosophical narratives which explore ideas by placing their protagonist in ethical, religious or metaphysical dilemmas such as ibn Shahid's (d.1075) **al-Tawabi** and al Maari's **Risalah al-Ghufran**.

The Thousand and One Nights, popular bawdy tales, not a literary masterpiece. But much used and abused by Western writers.

Ibn Tufayl (d.1185), physician, philosopher and author of one of the earliest philosophical novels, **The Life of Hayy**. Much plagiarised but seldom acknowledged. Defoe's **Robinson Crusoe** is a racist replica of the sublime Hayy.

Abu Nawas (d.810), master poet, scoundrel, companion and court jester of 'good Haroun Alraschid' in the **Arabian Nights**, and lover of wine:

> Ho! A cup and fill it up, and tell me it is wine,
> For never will I drink in shade if I can drink in shine.
> Curst and poor is every hour that sober I must go,
> But rich am I whene'er will drunk I stagger to and fro.
> Speak, for shame, the loved one's name, let vain disguises fall,
> Good for naught are pleasures hid behind a curtain-wall.

IS IT NECESSARY TO QUOTE THIS AWFUL POEM?

THE POETRY OF NATURE WAS PIONEERED BY IBN HAMDIS (d.1132), WHO HAS BEEN CALLED 'ARABIC WORDSWORTH'.

A unique institution of Muslim civilization was **Adab** or literature of manners and aphorisms. This offered the cream of what had been said in verse, prose, aphorism and pithy anecdote on every conceivable subject. One of the first adab works was ibn al-Muqaffa's (d. 757) moralizing animal fables of Bidpai, **Kalila wa-Dimna**. The archetypal representative of adab literature is al-Jahiz (d.868) 'the goggle eyed'. His masterpiece **The Book of Animals** is still widely read.

THE FIRST SERIAL PART WORKS AND ENCYCLOPEDIAS WERE PIONEERED NOT BY MARSHALL CAVENDISH BUT BY THE BRETHREN OF PURITY CIRCA 983.

Science

The scientific achievements of Muslim civilization are truly staggering. Indeed, scientific method, as generally understood today, was introduced by the great Muslim empiricists and experimenters. In the lab reports of al-Battani (d. 929), al-Baruni (d.1048) and ibn Haytham (d.1039) we find this method described and used. The Muslims also turned mathematics into the language of science. With these two innovations there seemed no limit to their research and discoveries.

The earliest breakthroughs took place in mathematics and astronomy. Al-Khwarizmi (d. 850) invented logarithms and algebra which comes from the title of book **Kitab al-jabr wa' muqabala** (The Book of Inheritance). Through this book, 300 year later, the Western world would be introduced to the zero and adopt Arabic numerals. In **The Shape of the Earth**, al-Khwarizmi left no one in doubt. Abdul Wafa (d. 997/8) developed trigonometry and spherical geometry, came up with sine and tangent tables, and discovered variations in the moon's motion. Omar Khayyam (d.1123) solved third and fourth-degree equations by intersecting conics - the highest algebraic achievement of modern mathematics.

OMAR KHAYYAM, MEDIOCRE POET, BRILLIANT MATHEMATICIAN.

So accurate were Muslim scientists that al-Battani, considered to be the greatest Islamic astronomer, was out only by 24 seconds from today's accepted value in his calculation of the length of the solar year. Al-Baruni's measurements of specific gravities of various metals and precious stones and of longitude and latitudes of earth are correct to three decimal places.

FIVE HUNDRED YEARS BEFORE GALILEO, AL-BARUNI DISCUSSED THE ROTATION OF THE EARTH ON ITS AXIS; AND AL-BATTANI MEASURED THE CIRCUMFERENCE OF THE EARTH!

The planetary orbit according to al-Bitruji: the orbit of the planet is a sphere or globe, which turns on its axis, the pole of which rotates around another axis, so that the planet produces a loop-like movement.

Planet

Ibn al-Haytham (d.1039) was a trailblazer in optics. Experimenting with 27 different types of spherical lenses, he discovered the laws of reflection and refraction, explained the apparent increase in the size of the stars near the zenith, and discovered that the eye does not send out rays (as Euclid and Ptolemy believed) but reflects them. His **Optical Thesaurus** is one of the most plagiarised texts in the history of science. Guilty parties include Roger Bacon, da Vinci, Kepler; even Newton is under scholarly suspicion.

Use of a kamal to measure the altitude of the pole star, from which the latitude could be calculated.

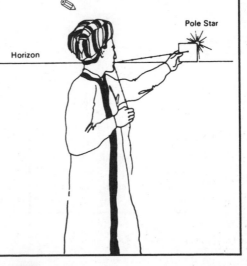

Pole Star

Horizon

At the numerous observatories throughout the Muslim world, astronomical tables were prepared and published by countless astronomers, each checking, correcting and improving the tables of his predecessor. Some of them published reference books on stars, even differentiating between stars and nebulae. The observatories at Maraga, Damascus, al-Rayy, Seville and Samarkand were amongst the most famous. At Maraga, where the special attraction was a quadrant of ten feet radius, the famous astronomer al-Tusi (d.1274) worked on planetary motion. His work was continued by ibn ash-Shatir (d.1375) at Damascus.

Historians of science have noticed the similarity between the planetary models produced at Maraga and Damascus with those of Copernicus. A mere coincidence?

Astronomy comes immediately after religion as the most noble and perfect science. It adorns the mind and sharpens the intellect, it makes man recognize God's oneness. – Al-Battani in **Opus Astronomicium**.

✍ *Thabit bin Qurra's (d. 901) theory of 'trepidation': superimposed on the uniform recession, the zero point of the ecliptic describes a small circle of 4 degrees radius in 4000 years.*

Praise be to Allah for He has not provided wings for the horse or our roofs would have come tumbling down.

Chemistry too received a grounding in experimental method. Jabir ibn Hayyan (d. 813) invented numerous types of laboratory apparatus, introduced distillation for the purification of water, identified numerous alkalis, acids, salts, prepared sulphuric acid, caustic soda and nitrohydrochloric acid for dissolving metals and discovered mercury. Abu Bakr Al-Razi (d. 935) divided chemical substances into categories of mineral, vegetable and animal and declared that the functions of the human body were based on complex chemical reactions.

JABIR EVEN DEVELOPED PAINT FOR COMMERCIAL USE.

JABIR LUX PAINT

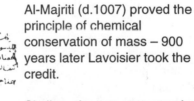

Al-Majriti (d.1007) proved the principle of chemical conservation of mass – 900 years later Lavoisier took the credit.

Similar advances were made in botany, zoology and other natural sciences. Al-Jahiz (d. 869) wrote the first comprehensive zoological study: **The Animals**. Kamal ad-Din ad-Damiri (d.1405) developed the idea of zoological taxonomy in his **The Life of Animals**. Abu Bakr al-Baytar (d.1340) produced one the most comprehensive works on veterinary medicine in **Kamil as-Sina'atayn**.

In 1121, Al-Khazini published his **Book of the Balance of Wisdom**. Apart from a detailed discussion of techniques of measurement and construction of balances, laws of mechanics, hydrostatics and physics, the book also contains a number of theories – a theory of solids, a theory of the behaviour of levers and a theory that identifies a universal central force directed towards the centre of the earth. Newton's apple would fall 566 years later!

A few Arabic words in common scientific parlance:
azimuth, zenith, nadir
star names: like Betelgeose
(**bait al-Jauzah**) and Algol (**ra's al-ghul**)
chemistry – **al-kimiya**
alcohol – **al-kuhol**
alkaline – **al-qalawi**
arsenic – **al-zirnich**.

Al-Farghani's (d.870), **The Elements of Astronomy**, which deals mainly with celestial motion, was freely used by Dante in his **Vita Nuova**, **Convivio** and **The Divine Comedy**.

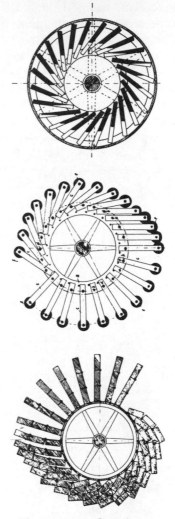

Three perpetual-motion machines described in a chapter on water-wheels written some time between the ninth and twelfth centuries AD.

Technology

T he development of technology in the Muslim civilization was intimately connected with crafts and professional industries. The distillation of rose-water, perfumes, and the scented oils in plants and flowers – the 'essential oils' – was a gigantic industry. Technology for producing and distilling crude petroleum was developed as early as the ninth century as the excellent description in al-Razi's **Book of the Secret of Secrets** shows so clearly. Also developed by this time were technologies for extraction of industrial oils and fats, preparation of acids, manufacture of soap and glass, ceramics, inks, pigments, dyes, paper and leather goods. The history of water power, including the construction of dams and windmills, begins with Islamic culture.

The Book of Ingenious Devices by the three Banu Musa brothers, who flourished in Baghdad during the ninth century, describes one hundred working machines, 75 being their own inventions.

A self-replenishing vessel described in Kitab al-hiyal by Banu Musa brothers.

A number of innovative irrigation technologies were introduced by the Muslims, including the water-wheel and the technique for the utilization of subterranean water by means of underground conduits called **qanats**. Countless machines, using gears, cranks and pistons for raising water from the ground for irrigation, drinking and domestic uses, were invented.

Muslims also developed surveying techniques, underground mining (complete with miner's lamp) and technologies for manufacturing alloys and steel.

In his twelfth century **Compendium of the Theory and Practice of the Mechanical Arts**, al-Jazari says that any industrial science which is not verified by experiments is a doubtful science, and gives careful descriptions of calibration procedures.

انّيَة اعنى ان لايَبطفى النار ويكون اية الوقودية انبوب النار وهم المجوس

IS THIS A LAMP?

Top: Scoop wheel by the river.
Left: A miner's lamp with a pivoted sheild, described by the Musa brothers. The sheild was designed so it would be turned by the wind to the position where it would protect the lamp.

وفي البيع وهم النصارى وان جعلت المنارة وخزانة الزيت جملة

Muslims excelled in making accurate instruments. The planispheric astrolabe, the earliest analogue computer, is a purely Islamic invention. It was the most powerful tool available to astronomers before the advent of modern instruments. With it, one could determine the times of rising, setting and culmination of the Sun and stars, find the position of a celestial body at a given time, as well as solve a number of other astronomical problems. In Taqi al-Din's **The Brightest Stars for the Construction of Mechanical Clocks**, written in 1565, we find a detailed description for the construction of a clock with verge-and-foliot escapement, a striking train of gears, an alarm, and a representation of the moon's phases. Also in the same manual is a description of a spring-driven clock.

The first planispheric astrolabe was constructed by Al-Fazari (d.790?).

Medicine

Medicine was developed to an astonishingly high degree by Muslims. The first organized hospital was built for lepers in Damascus. Soon afterwards every Muslim city had its own central hospital. Baghdad alone had 60 hospitals. These hospitals were remarkably advanced in design and contained pharmacies, libraries, lecture-rooms for medical students, separate wards for men and women and facilities for out-patients.

صُوَرَةِ طَبِيبُ وَشَكِلَّآتَ وَصُورَةِ عَلِيـنِ بُوْنكَرُدِنِ .

Engraving from a treatise on surgery.

The greatest Muslim physician was undoubtedly al-Razi (d.925). His descriptions of the clinical signs of many illnesses are unsurpassed. He investigated women's diseases and established midwifery, wrote on hereditary diseases, eye diseases and gave the first account of smallpox and measles. Many of the ideas and concepts contained in his 24 volume encyclopedia on medicine, **al-Hawi – The Continence** – are still valid today!

Ibn Sina's (d.1037) **The Canons of Medicine**, in 14 volumes, was a standard medical text in the West for 700 years! It deals with diseases, their classification, description, and causes, with therapeutics and descriptions of simple and compound medicines, with hygiene, the functions of parts of the body and numerous other topics. Ibn Sina noted that tuberculosis was contagious and described the symptoms and complications of diabetes. He was very interested in the effect of the mind on the body and wrote a great deal on psychology.

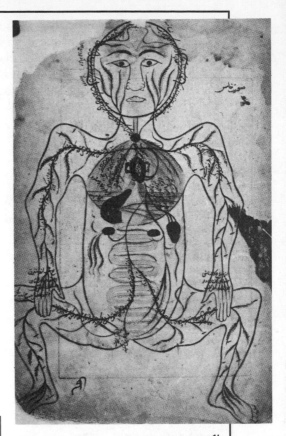

IBN NAFIS (d. 1288) FIRST ACCURATELY DESCRIBED THE CIRCULATION OF BLOOD THROUGH THE BODY — IN 1628 THE CREDIT WENT TO HARVEY!

✍ *Drawings of surgical instruments, from a treatise on external pathology by az-Zahrawi. Sixteenth century manuscript from Morocco.*

One of the more famous manuals on surgery was written by Al-Zahrawi (b. 939). Apart from descriptions of how to perform a whole variety of operations, **Al-Tasrif** includes detailed descriptions of over a hundred surgical instruments – many al-Zahrawi's own inventions. He also developed dentistry and performed cosmetic operations to correct dental irregularities.

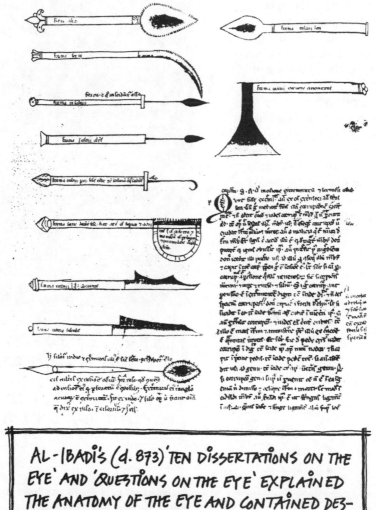

AL-IBADI'S (d. 873) 'TEN DISSERTATIONS ON THE EYE' AND 'QUESTIONS ON THE EYE' EXPLAINED THE ANATOMY OF THE EYE AND CONTAINED DESCRIPTIONS OF THE BRAIN AND OPTIC NERVE.

Social Sciences

The Muslims also infused the critical spirit of inquiry into social sciences. History, including archaeology and ethnology, was a Muslim vocation above all others. The monumental works of universal history by al-Tabri, al-Masudi, al-Athir and ibn Khaldun show the quantum leap that history received from Muslim civilization.

All records, by their very nature, are liable to error...

☛ *the first of these is partisanship towards a creed or opinion...*

☛ *the second factor...is over-confidence in one's sources...*

☛ *the third is the failure to understand what is intended...*

☛ *the fourth is a mistaken belief in the truth...*

☛ *the fifth is the inability to place an event in its real context...*

☛ *the sixth is the common desire to gain favour of those of*

high ranks, by praising them, by spreading their fame...

☛ *the seventh, and the most important, is the ignorance of the laws*

governing the transformations of human society.

Ibn Khaldun in **The Muqadimmah**

Psychology was a well-established discipline in the Muslim civilization with such eminent psychologists as ibn Sina and ibn Tufayl. But the greatest Muslim psychologist is the Sufi philosopher, poet and musician, ibn Bajjah (d.1138) whose **The Book of Ego** influenced countless Muslim authors.

Al-Mawardi (d.1058) introduced an original theory of the state in his **Book on the Principles of Government** and ibn Taymiyya's (d.1317) numerous writings on political theory established the basis for a Muslim political science. Ibn Taymiyya's rigorous works on comparative religion were not always pleasing to the Shia or the Christians.

Geography and Travel

ravel was a big business in the Muslim civilization. Muslim ships sailed to every part of the known world and Muslim scientists developed charts and maps of the sea areas divided into squares of longitude and latitude containing directions of prevailing winds and data about tidal conditions. A sophisticated system of postal services was introduced as early as the tenth century. The adventures of **Sindbad the Sailor** reflect the realities of commerce and communications during the Abbasid period.

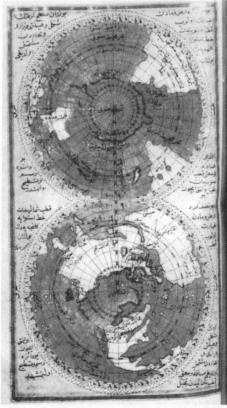

The swashbuckling adventures in the Volga-Caspian regions of the 10th century traveller ibn Fadlan make riveting reading and provide one of the earliest accounts of this area.

ibn Battuta (d.1369):
I visited the lands of every Muslim ruler of my time and travelled to China, Sri Lanka, Byzantium and South Russia.

One of the earliest geographical works is **Routes and Kingdoms** by ibn Khuradadhbih published in 848. Apart from the Muslim empire, it provides descriptions of such distant areas as China, Korea and Japan. Exactly a hundred years later, al-Masudi published his famous geographical encyclopedia, **Meadows of Gold and Mines of Precious Stones**.

...which amongst other things, discusses earthquakes, geological formations and the nature of the Dead Sea.

Al-Masudi's later works discuss geological evolution. In 1154, al-Idris, one of the most renowned Muslim geographers and cartographers, published the first spherical, accurate and 'modern' map of the world and described the use of the compass in his book **Amusement for him who Desires to Travel Round the World**. Yaqut Hamawi's (d.1229) **Geographical Dictionary** lists, in alphabetical order, almost every known town and place and provides remarkably accurate information on the size of the earth, climatic zones and physical, mathematical and political geography.

Ibn Majid, who piloted Vasco de Gama from Africa to the Indian coast, published a manual on the art of navigation for pilots and mariners in rhymed prose in 1489.

Architecture and Town Planning

own planning was a sophisticated science in the Muslim civilization. Towns were usually built near a river which supplied drinking and domestic water (upstream) as well as carrying away waste and sewage (down stream and underground). Muslims introduced the idea of carrying capacity and built towns for a calculated number of families. They also introduced the idea of **haram**, inviolate zones – outside towns, near water-courses and other areas – where development was forbidden.

Architects with their instruments.

CREATIVE LOT WERE'NT THEY?

As the basic formation, the courtyard determined the shape and size of each house, which in turn interrelated with the grouping of houses to form a neighbourhood. The resultant compact and continuous layout of buildings reduced land waste to a minimum and provided a network of cool alleyways and squares. Different professions, craftsmen and artisans were grouped in different locations and a sense of community was maintained through a network of compact and highly dense neighbourhoods. The mosques and colleges were both physically and spiritually at the centre of the town, with the suqs as the centre of commercial and social life. The narrow and steep alleyways and covered passages made it possible to walk everywhere in the town.

This is how the historic towns of Baghdad, Damascus, Tunis, Fez, Algiers, Sana, Lahore, Herat, Dubai, Istanbul, Aleppo and Cairo were designed and laid out.
▼

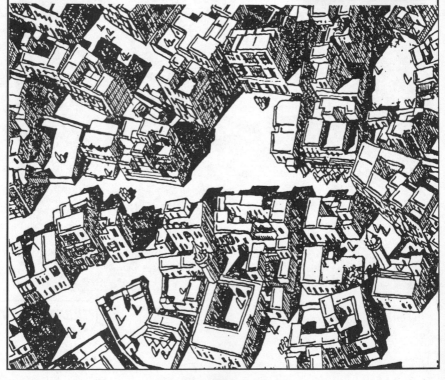

The Muslims also introduced **hima**, a second kind of inviolate zone, solely for the conservation of wildlife and forests. There were five types of hima zones:

❀ **1.** reserves in which grazing was prohibited;

❀ **2.** reserves for forests in which cutting of trees was forbidden;

❀ **3.** reserves in which grazing was restricted to certain seasons;

❀ **4.** reserves for beekeeping in which grazing was forbidden during flowering; and

❀ **5.** reserves managed for the welfare of a particular village, town or tribe.

Ibn abd as-Salam, who flourished during the thirteenth century, formulated the first statement of animal rights.

Muslim architecture speaks for itself. Just look at the skyline of Istanbul, the Taj Mahal, al-Hamra in Granada, the mosque in Cordoba, the multi-storey mud houses of Sana, the whole city of Fez (almost intact as it was built circa 800), the Friday mosque in Larabanga, the wind tower houses in Dubai...the list is endless.

Art

Islamic art is one of the finest manifestations of Muslim civilization. Its most outstanding feature is the emphasis on calligraphy and decorative arts. Even today, calligraphy is the dominant Muslim art form. Quite naturally, it is the verses from the Qur'an that are used on religious as well as non-religious objects.

The emphasis on decorative art led to the development of pottery, tile making, metalwork, glass-cutting and enameling, ivory carving, bookbinding – all reached the highest artistic peaks. Economically, the most important were the textile crafts such as cloth-making, carpet knotting and tapestry weaving. Book illustration, illumination and miniature paintings were popular amongst the educated classes. Not all the arts flourished at the same time or in the same place – they span a vast geographical as well as historic range.

Music

Muslims classified music as a mathematical science, and numerous mathematicians, philosophers and mystics wrote treatises on music. But the most famous work on the theory of music is by Safi al-Din (1294).

The 'classical' system of music was championed by al-Mawsili (d.850). His student, the master

musician Ziryab, introduced this system to Spain in 822. The most outstanding contribution of the Muslim theorists was the development of **mensural** music, introduced to Europe in the twelfth century, before which measured song was unknown to the West. Equally important was the concept of **gloss** or adornment of a melody. It was a type of gloss known as the **tarkib**, the striking of a note simultaneously with its fourth or fifth octave, that gave Europe the idea of **harmony**.

EAT YOUR HEART OUT MICHAEL!

The development of the theory and practice of music produced numerous instruments. A whole family of stringed instruments of the lute, pendore and guitar group, and the bowed instrument of various types, originated in the Muslim civilization and were passed on to the West via Spain. With the stringed instruments came the places of the notes fixed on the finger-board by means of **fiet** or **farida** which were determined by measurement. – Before that, European minstrals only had **cithara** and harps among their instruments and were guided merely by their ears in tuning.

Spread of Muslim Learning to Europe

U p to the 16th century, the flow of knowledge was strictly from Islam to Europe. The works of Muslim scholars were regularly translated into Latin and other European languages, used as text books and practical manuals. European scholars and thinkers were regular visitors at Muslim centres of learning. European students went to Cardova, Fez, Cairo, Baghdad, Samarkand to study under great masters' just as Muslim students nowadays come to Europe and North America for further study. Arabic was the language of science and culture, and those who cared for thought and learning showed their concern by dressing like Muslim scholars.

The European Renaissance and all the progress in science, technology, medicine, learning and humanism that it produced, was built squarely on the shoulders of Muslim scholars and thinkers. Indeed, the Renaissance is inconceivable without the contribution of Muslim civilization. This fact is seldom acknowledged. On the contrary, the achievements of Muslim scholars and scientists were frequently plagiarized, deliberately and systematically downgraded, undermined and brushed aside.

✎ How to argue (specially philosophically): intellectual methods

✎ Greek philosophy: Plato, Aristotle and the Neoplatonists, Empirical and Experimental Method

✎ University system (lock, stock and barrel – including the chair)

✎ How to count: zero, Arabic numerals

✎ Algebra, trigonometry and spherical geometry

✎ Laboratory tools: test tubes, flasks and the like.

✎ Optics, the basic laws of light

✎ Hospitals, surgical tools

✎ Bibliographical Tools: catalogues, bibliographies, dictionaries, biographical dictionaries, thesauri, encyclopedias

✎ Organization and administration of libraries; classification schemes

✎ Paper manufacture

✎ Publishing (as a mass industry) and bookshops

✎ Hydrology; various irrigational tools

✎ How to find your way: calculation of direction; navigation, compass

✎ Cartography: an authentic map of the world

✎ Basic set of astronomical facts and laws (most of which were plagiarized)

✎ Basic understanding of the human body

✎ The basic 'Canons of Medicine' (ibn Sina's and al-Razi's)

✎ Universal history (which was itself used to undermine Muslim history) Sociology

✎ How to be a mystic without freaking out

✎ The art of 'gracious living'

✎ Musical harmony; guitar and other stringed instruments and the technique of playing them!

A few things that the West failed to learn from Muslims (and which the Muslims themselves have forgotten)

That knowledge and values cannot be separated
When it is necessary to leave technology alone
The importance of holistic thought and action
Environmental husbandry: the notion of trusteeship, inviolate environmental zones
How to enjoy sex without feeling guilty*
Multiculturalism**

A PRIEST ATTEMPTING TO CONVERT MUSLIMS TO CHRISTIANITY.

CAN WE KEEP SEX OUT OF THIS BOOK!

*Too hot for a beginner's primer like this one. But see the much used and abused works of Shaikh Masumi's **The Perfumed Garden** written in the fifteen century and ibn Sulayman's **How an Old Man Can Become Young Again** published towards the end of the fourteenth century. See the **Fahirist** of al-Nadim for further references.

**Muslim Spain (750-1492) was the first, and the only, truly multireligious and multicultural society in history; Muslim Bosnia and Malaysia are contemporary examples of Islamic multiculturalism in action.

Decline

The decline of the Muslim civilization has been attributed to a number of factors. Internal divisions and feuds within the Muslim empire, the corrupt and luxuriant lifestyles of the rulers, the fall of Baghdad and the loss of Spain are commonly cited reasons for the downfall of the Musiims.

A LAME-DUCK ABBASID CALIPHATE WAS RE-ESTABLISHED IN CAIRO. AFTER THE OTTOMAN CONQUEST OF EGYPT IN 1517, ISTANBUL BECAME THE CENTRE OF THE MUSLIM EMPIRE.

When the Mongol hordes arrived at the gates of Baghdad in 1258, the Abbasids were too weak to defend the city. It was razed to the ground and everyone, including the caliph, was put to the sword. The intellectual loss was also devastating: the Mongols burnt astronomical numbers of manuscripts and destroyed all the libraries so painstakingly built by early Abbasid caliphs.

The second major blow came with the loss of Spain. Here events followed the same course as in Baghdad: internal feuds, divisions, corruption of rulers... When Boadbil, the Moorish Prince of Granada, knelt before King Ferdinand on 2 January 1492 and handed over the keys to the city of Granada, he ended 800 glorious and truly enlightening years of Muslim rule in Spain. Boabdil's mother rebuked her son with the words that have haunted Muslim history ever since.

You weep like a woman for what you could not hold as a man.

The intellectual loss was equally great: countless manuscripts were ritualistically burnt and centuries of Muslim learning were suppressed.

But the sack of Baghdad and the fall of Granada, though turning points in Muslim history, cannot really be considered as the main causes for Muslim decline. The force that placed Muslim civilization in reverse gear was an internal and conceptual one.

Towards the end of the 14th century, the **ulama** (religious scholars), who, thanks to al-Ghazzali, were in a position of dominance, began to conceive of the written word as an independent realm of representation and truth apart from life. The proliferation of books had created a distance between authors and the words that carried their ideas across space and time. The text was open to every variety of interpretation, irrespective of real facts and truth.

THIS IS BLATANTLY ANTI-MULLA.

So what if a given text is open to a number of interpretations? The **ulama** had two concerns. First, they were concerned that the Qur'an was open to all kinds of wild interpretations, not just by untutored readers, but also by theologically unqualified professional writers. To some extent, this was a genuine concern given the variety of irrational and exploitative behaviour that was being justified on the basis of the Qur'an and tradition. But this was intimately linked to the second and more important worry: the proliferation of written texts had began to undermine the authority and control that the ulama enjoyed over both the Muslim rulers and the masses.

It took the ulama over a hundred years to respond to the problem. Their response was threefold:

➤➤ **1.** They reduced the concept of **ilm** from meaning 'all knowledge' to mean only 'religious knowledge.'

➤➤ **2.** They transformed the concept of **ijma** from meaning 'the consensus of the community' to mean 'the consensus of the learned,' i.e. the consensus of the ulama themselves.

➤➤ **3.** And they closed 'the gates of **ijtihad**': independent reasoning on matters of religion was effectively outlawed.

This had a devastating effect on Muslim society. Ijtihad thus gave way to **taqlid** (blind imitation); reasoning, speculation and innovation were replaced by imitation. The interpretation of the Qur'an was frozen in history. In the absence of new ideas, reflection and understanding of changing circumstances, Muslim thought ossified and became totally obscurantist. Consequently, Muslim culture lost its dynamism and degenerated, while the Muslim community was transformed from an open to a closed society.

The religious scholars defended the highly privileged territory they created for themselves with great vigour. In sharp contrast to how rapidly the Muslims acquired paper from the Chinese and turned it into an industry, the ulama managed to resist the introduction of printing presses in Muslim countries for nearly three centuries. They argued that mass printing of books would lead not to the understanding and appreciation of sacred and classical texts but to their misrepresentation and misunderstanding in untutored hands. By 'forbidding' printing, the ulama deprived Muslim society of a crucial source of oxygen. The Muslim countries were now ready to be devoured by European powers.

Colonialism

ith minor variations, the European powers which colonized the Muslim world – Britain, France, Holland – behaved according to a set pattern. 'Divide and conquer' was the policy of occupation. For example, by playing off one ruler in India against another till exhausted, the British could easily devour the Mughal empire. The war of independence in 1857 was the last effort on the part of the Indian masses to overthrow the British. It failed miserably. Bahadar Shah Zafar, the last Mughal Emperor of India, was not very keen on 'free trade' and was reluctant to give the British trading concessions as he suspected their motives. His suspicions proved to be correct. As a first gesture of their intentions to civilize the natives, the British presented him with the heads of his entire family on silver platters. Zafar was exiled to Rangoon where he died in abject poverty and wrote some of the greatest poems in Urdu literature.

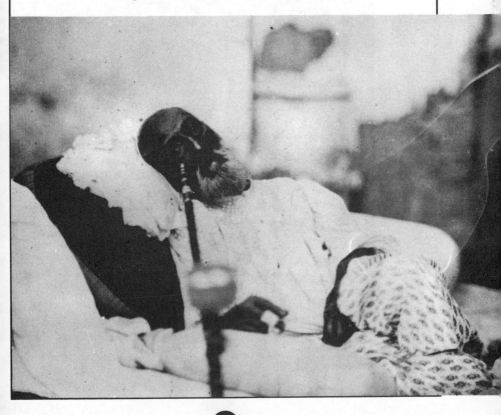

On taking control, colonial powers systematically stripped Muslim society of all its learning and expertise. One of the first acts of colonial rulers was to ban all intellectual, learned and educational activities. For example, when the Dutch took over Indonesia in 1595, they closed all **madrasas**, colleges and libraries and banned education. Natives were forbidden from entering the few libraries that the Dutch established for their own purposes. In 1850, they allowed primary education for the natives but still prohibited secondary education. The destruction of Islamic medicine came next. At the beginning of the nineteenth century, a French doctor needed permission to practice medicine in Tunisia from the Muslim Chief of Physicians. By the end of the century, French colonial administrators classed Islamic medicine as second rate and then proceeded ruthlessly to suppress it. Eventually, Islamic medicine was outlawed all over the Muslim world.

Manufacturing Colonialism

The colonial powers looted everything they could from the Muslim societies they colonized, and most established a structure for transferring all the local raw material to the 'mother country'.

MY PRINCE AND MY COUNTRY

THE TEXTILE MILLS OF NORTHERN ENGLAND, FOR EXAMPLE, WERE BUILT ON THE RUINS OF THE INDIAN TEXTILE INDUSTRY. COLONIALISM AND THE 'INDUSTRIAL REVOLUTION' WERE LOCKED TOGETHER.

The European rulers created a special class, generally of civil servants, as their local surrogates. Macaulay echoed other colonial rulers when he wrote in 1835 in his **Minutes of Indian Education** : 'We must at present do our best to form a class who may be interpreters between us and the millions whom we govern; a class of persons, Indian in blood and colour, but English in taste, in opinion, in morals, and in intellect.'

The British **East India Company** and the Dutch **East Indies Company** were free market ventures in the Muslim world. They were given concessions by various Muslim rulers to trade freely. But their trade included conquests and annexations. Today, **East India Company** T-shirts make a fashion statement.

Muslim societies became an experimental ground where all sorts of ideas of 'brave new modernists', missionaries with civilizing zeal, believers in science, progress and 'White Man's burden', tested out new, utopian and innovative educational, social and cultural policies on Muslim societies.

Colonialism dismantled Muslim civilization brick by brick. It occupied not only the bodies but also the 'minds' of Muslims. It equated anything that could remotely be described as Islamic with inferiority and low moral worth. It altered the cultural priorities of Muslim societies. It drained the Muslim countries of every source of wealth. And it reduced the Muslim people to abject poverty.

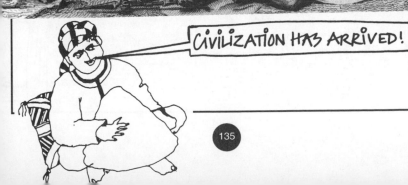

CIVILIZATION HAS ARRIVED!

Islam and the West

Muslims became a 'problem' for Europe right from the birth of Islam. First, Islam was a theological problem. What was the purpose of an Arabian Prophet some 600 years after the crucifixion and resurrection of God's own son? Second, when Islam arrived – within a few decades of its inception – at Europe's borders, it became a political problem. Third, the scholarly achievements of Muslim civilization made Islam an intellectual problem as well.

Each aspect of the problem of Islam was tackled by specific means. Theologically, Christian Europe could only denounce Islam, its Prophet and its followers. Politically, Europe launched a series of Crusades against Islam. When these failed, it embarked on full-fledged colonization of the Muslim world. Intellectually, it created a series of disciplines to contain Muslim thought and history.

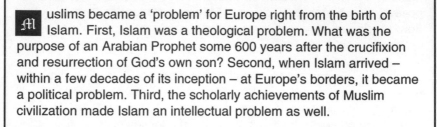

THE

GREAT HISTORICAL PICTURE

OF THE

STORMING OF **SERINGAPATAM,**

By the BRITISH TROOPS and their ALLIES, MAY 4th, 1799.

PAINTED by ROBERT KER PORTER.

DESCRIPTIVE SKETCH.

1. Denunciation

Denunciation of Islam and its Prophet began early on. Paul Alvarus (d.859) used the Book of Daniel to discover that Muhammad fitted the description of the Antichrist, complete with the sign of the beast 666, which was supposed to be the year of the Prophet's death. This defamatory picture of the Prophet was incorporated in the cycle of popular performance literature known as **chansons de geste** – where the Prophet is given the Devil's synonym, **Mahound** – and the epic romances that later developed out of them. Throughout the middle ages, they exerted tremendous influence on Italian, German, Spanish, French and English literature, surviving right up to the 17th century in different forms. The genre made a come back in the 19th and 20th centuries. The most recent example of the genre is Salman Rushdie's **The Satanic Verses** which rewrites the life of Prophet Muhammad in the defamatory style of **chansons** literature.

The terms "Muslim" and "fanatic" have often been synonymous in the European mind. Illustrated above a lithograph of 1880.

2. The Crusades

nce Islam was cast in the permanent role of demonic infidel enemy, perpetual war against it was relatively easy to justify. At the famous 'Peace of God' Council of Clermond in November 1095, Pope Urban II launched the crusades. The Council called for a 'War of God' against Islam and the liberation of Jerusalem.

When Omar, the Second Caliph, captured Jerusalem in 638, he treated the Christians and Jews with utmost respect. No one was harmed. When Omar met the Christian Patriarch, he assured him that the life and property of the city's inhabitant's would be respected and then asked to be taken to Christian holy places. During the visit, the time of prayer arrived when they were in the Church of the Holy Sepulchre. Omar asked the Patriarch's permission to pray. The Patriarch invited Omar to do so right where he stood. Omar answered: 'If I do, the Muslims would want to appropriate this site, saying "Omar prayed here". Then, with his prayer mat in his hand, Omar walked outside and prayed on naked ground.

The crusades began with the slaughter of the Jews in Europe. The crusaders entered Jerusalem, after a 40 day siege, on 15 July 1099. They killed some 70,000 men, women and children according to the Muslim historian ibn al-Athir. Listen to Raymund Aguiles, an eye-witness reporter ☞

The Jews of Jerusalem faced the same fate. And also their fellow Christians: Greeks, Copts, Syrians, Armenians and Georgians were taken out of the Church of the Holy Sepulchre, rounded up and tortured. Elsewhere in the Holy Land, the crusaders boiled Muslims in cooking pots, roasted children on spits and roamed the countryside hunting for 'pagan Saracens'.

Wonderful sights were to be seen. Some of our men (and this was more merciful) cut off the heads of their enemies; others shot them with arrows, so that they fell from the towers; others tortured them longer by casting them into flames. Piles of heads, hands and feet were to be seen in the streets of the city. It was necessary to pick one's way over the bodies of men and horses. But these were small matters compared to what happened at the Temple of Solomon, a place where religious services are normally chanted. What happened there? If I tell the truth it will exceed the powers of belief. So let it suffice to say this much, at least, that in the Temple and porch of Solomon, men rode in blood up to their knees and bridle reins. Indeed it was a just and splendid judgement of God that this place should be filled with the blood of the unbelievers since it had suffered so long from their blasphemies.

The Muslims recaptured Jerusalem on 2 October 1187. When the Ayyubid Caliph **Salah-ad-Din** (Saladin) entered the city, he gave strict orders to his troop that no Christian shall be touched. He announced that Christian holy places would be protected and that anyone who wished to stay could stay and anyone who wished to leave could leave. Many left and took their (looted) wealth with them.

The patriarch of Jerusalem himself raided the Church of the Holy Sepulchre and drove out of the city with numerous chariots filled with gold, carpets and all varieties of precious goods. The companions of Salah-ad-Din were scandalized. Imam al-Din al-Asfahani, Salah-ad-Din's treasurer, was beside himself with rage (☞ ↗

I said to the sultan: 'This patriarch is carrying off riches worth at least two hundred thousand dinars. We gave them permission to take their personal property with them, but not the treasures of the churches and the convents. You must not let them do it.' But Salah al-Din answered: 'We must apply the letter of the accords we have signed, so that no one will be able to accuse the believers of having violated their treaties. On the contrary, Christians everywhere will remember the kindness we have bestowed upon them.

CHRISTIANS EVERYWHERE PAINTED SALAH-AD-DIN AS A VIOLENT INFIDEL, WHO ATE BABIES, KILLED CHRISTIAN KNIGHTS AND DESTROYED CHRISTIAN HOLY PLACES!

The crusaders have had a tremendous influence on Europe's perception of Islam. The crusades projected Islam as the evil, dark side of Europe. This stereotype picture of Muslims as barbaric, licentious, depraved, fanatical, ignorant, stupid, unclean and inferior, became an integral part of European thought, literature and outlook. It was sustained and developed under colonialism and is periodically recycled in our time.

3. Orientalism

Special disciplines evolved to provide academic justification for false images of Islam. Anthropology emerged to study all non-Western cultures as the imperfect and **primitive** versions of Western society. Islam received the expected racist treatment at the hands of many colonial anthropologists. **Orientalism** was developed specifically to cast the fear and loathing of Islam into an acceptable objective and academic framework.

Orientalist writers, who have often tended to be priests, have since the 15th century been rewriting Islamic history, presenting perversely grotesque descriptions of Islamic sources, attributing wicked and innately evil characteristics to Muslim societies. The Qur'an was repeatedly analysed as a incoherent, repetitious, violent book of little consequence. Muhammad was constantly presented as amoral and licentious. Muslim thought and learning was suppressed and written out of the history of science!

Orientalism was/is not just an academic pursuit – it was/is also an outlook towards Islam. European travellers, novelists and artists have produced a vast corpus of literature and paintings depicting Islam as a barbaric fusion of sex and violence, a treasure house of magic, superstition, drugs and deformations. Many of these writers – such as Richard Burton (d.1890), Isabelle Eberhardt (d.1904), T E Lawrence (d.1935) – went to the Muslim world either as spies or to seek sexual gratification denied them in Europe.

Sensuality and sex ooze from this languorous Algerian odalisque by Renoir. The harem and its delights were a frequent resort for the imagination of 19th century painters and writers. Renoir painted this in 1870, nine years before he visited Algiers.

The Western attempts to solve the 'problem' of Islam have produced a catalogue of crimes and injustices against Muslims that defies description.

It has led to an institutionalization of Islam and Muslims as the **Demonised Other** in European thought and history.

It has perverted Western scholarship on Islam and the exploration of Muslim societies in literature and travel.

THIS IS HENRI REGNAULT'S CONTRIBUTION. ▶

But beyond the stereotypes and clichés of European history, Muslims are working to rebuild their ransacked civilization.

Reform and Revival

M uslim struggles against European imperialism began almost immediately with the dawn of colonialism. But traditional revolts which had proved so effective in early Muslim history were no match for European military technology and administrative capabilities. Muslim thinkers thus sought to fight colonialism by revitalizing Islam and uniting the Muslim world.

One of the earliest attempts to reverse the decline of Islam was undertaken in the Arabian peninsula by Mohammad ibn Abd al-Wahhab (d.1787). Abd al-Wahhab united the warring Arabian tribes and established a modern state in Arabia. He preached a simple return to faith and obedience to the fundamental teachings of Islam combined with discipline, piety and a sense of sacrifice. His son-in-law, Mohammad ibn Saud, gave his name to modern Saudi Arabia.

In the Indian subcontinent, the Sufi scholar, Shah Wali Allah (d.1763), made the first attempt to rethink the entire system of Islam in a spirit of objectivity. His emphasis on social justice combined with popular mysticism, gained him an enormous following. Shah Wali Allah stressed the essential unity of all religions and tried to develop a modern Islamic philosophy of history.

Similar reforms and anti-imperialist movements emerged throughout the Muslim world. In the Sudan, Mohammad Ahmad, known to his followers as the Mahdi (d.1885), fought the British in a series of battles and succeeded in setting up an Islamic state in the Sudan. In Libya, Muhammad Ali al-Sanusi (1859) founded the Sanusi Order for the rejuvenation and reform of Islam. In Algeria, Amir Abd al-Qadir (1884), established the Ulama Movement which fought both for reform of Muslim society and against the French colonists. In Nigeria, Osman dan Fadio (d.1817) led a revolutionary movement and succeeded in establishing the Sukoto Caliphate. In British India, Sir Sayyid Ahmad Khan (d.1898) emphasized selective adaptation of western political ideas and technical innovations and established the celebrated Aligarh Muslim University.

The tomb of Muhammad Ahmad.

In the late 19th century, pan-Islamism emerged to cut across ethnic and tribal affiliations and combine the efforts of the regional movements to create an international Islamic force. Its main proponent was Jalamuddin Afghani (d.1897). Dubbed 'the wild man of genius', Afghani sought to modernize Islam and exhorted Muslims everywhere to rise against European imperialism.

Afghani combined his reform work with Muhammad Abduh (d.1905), the Grand Mufti of Egypt, and together they edited an influential Arabic weekly, **Urwat al-Wuthqa** (The Indissoluble Link), which shaped the ideas and ideals of a whole generation of Muslim intellectuals. The movement that emerged from their efforts to give a modern identity to Islam, and provide Muslim societies with purpose and direction, came to be known as Salafism.

REFORMERS, REFORMERS EVERYWHERE. WHERE IS THE REFORM?

Liberation movements everywhere were inspired by 'the poet-philosopher of the East', Muhammad Iqbal (d.1938). His poetry, philosophic genius and passionate vision of Islamic revival based on social justice and elevated believers struck a chord with Muslims throughout the world. Iqbal argued that dogmatism had debased Islam, territorial and racial nationalism had split Muslims into aggressive groups, and materialistic philosophy was taking everyone towards nihilism. Iqbal's vision led to the creation of Pakistan and his philosophy has become a benchmark for all reformist thought in modern Islam.

آزادئ افکار سے ہے ان کی تباہی
رکھتے نہیں جو فکر و تدبّر کا سلیقہ

The thirties saw the emergence of two of the most influential Islamic organizations in the Muslim world. In Egypt, Hasan al-Banna (d.1949), a school teacher, established **Ikhwan al Muslimin** or the Muslim Brotherhood. Abu'l Ala Mawdudi (d.1979), a journalist, established the **Jamaat-e-Islami** in India.

The Muslim Brotherhood is committed to religious, political and intellectual reform of Islam. Its message of returning to the Islamic roots, re-establishing the Madina state of the Prophet Muhammad in our time, found favour with young Muslims. But in 1947, the Brotherhood was accused of political terrorism and disbanded. Two years later Hasan al-Banna himself was murdered.

In 1952, Jamal Abdul Nasser, enlisted the support of the Muslim Brotherhood to overthrow King Farouk. When in power, Nasser turned against the Brotherhood and persecuted them ruthlessly. Hundreds of its members were imprisoned without trial and tortured.

It was in prison that Syyed Qutb, the intellectual leader of the movement, wrote many of his influential works, such as **Social Justice in Islam**. In 1966, along with five other leading figures of the Brotherhood, Syyed Qutb was executed by President Nasser. He was accused of writing a seditious work: **Milestones**. The book argues that Muslims are living in an age of ignorance and their salvation, in this world and the Hereafter, lies in returning to the roots of Islam.

THE MUSLIM BROTHERHOOD HAS CONSIDERABLE INFLUENCE IN EGYPT, THE SUDAN, JORDAN, SYRIA AND ELSEWHERE IN THE ARAB WORLD.

After partition between India and Pakistan, Jamaat-e-Islami emerged as an Islamic party devoted to the establishment of an **Islamic state** in Pakistan. It fought several elections in Pakistan, but it has never gained more than a handful of seats in the parliament. It collaborated with General Ziaul Haq and, for a short period, was a partner in his government.

Mawdudi is one of the most widely read Muslim thinkers today and has a guru status amongst Muslim activists in many countries. By far the most important of his numerous books is **Caliphate and Monarchy**, an original and brave attempt at a reinterpretation of the early history of Islam. Conservative and puritan, Mawdudi's thought is complex, often moving between flashes of brilliance to statements of shallow piety, between radical diagnosis of Muslim malaise to naive solutions.

Islamic parties in Malaysia, Indonesia, Turkey, Afghanistan and the Sudan are influenced by Jamaat-e-Islami.

After the death of their founders and intellectual mentors, both the Jamaat-e-Islami and the Muslim Brotherhood have become intellectually sterile. While they command tremendous allegiance, they have lost much of their intellectual credibility.

BOTH ORGANIZATIONS ARE HIGHLY DISCIPLINED, EXTREMELY WELL ORGANIZED AND OPERATE AS CLOSED INSTITUTIONS.

The Muslim World

uring the forties and fifties many Muslim countries gained their independence. The contemporary Muslim world straddles the global middle belt: from the shores of Senegal and Morocco to the Pacific Ocean and the islands of Indonesia, and north to south from the Mediterranean coast of Turkey to Somalia. The Muslim world consists of some 52 sovereign states at various stages of development, incorporating more than 60 languages and with ethnic backgrounds as diverse as those of the Arabs and Indians, the Turks and the Pathans, the Chinese and the Malays, the Uzbek and the Hausa.

The end of the cold war gave independence to six new Muslim states in Central Asia : Uzbekistan, Kazakhstan, Kyrgyzstan, Turkmenistan, Tajikistan and Azerbaijan. In Europe, Albania shed its Stalinist past and Bosnia-Herzegovina broke away from former Yugoslavia and was invaded by the Serbians.

Muslim Minorities

The global Muslim community, or the **ummah**, is much more than just the Muslim world. Its a supranational entity with a common religious culture and history and a certain consciousness of belonging together. One-third of the ummah exists as minorities in non-Muslim countries.

The Muslims of India – consisting of over 120 million people – are the world's largest minority.

Over 60 million Muslims live in China. And there are large Muslim minorities in the Philippines, Burma, Thailand and Sri Lanka.

Immigration

ince the fifties, after the independence of many Muslim countries, Muslims have been migrating to the West. In Europe, this migration took place on a well-established route. Families from all over the Muslim world sought to make new homes in the countries of their former colonial masters. Thus, Muslims from India, Pakistan and Bangladesh came to Britain. Algerians, Moroccons and Tunisians went to France. Indonesians and Surinames went to Holland. The relationship between Turkey and Germany during the wars led to the establishment of a substantial Turkish community in Germany. There are now an estimated over 20 million Muslims living in Europe.

NOW WE HAVE TO SUFFER RACISM!

Black Muslims

ver the last decades, over 6 million Muslims have settled in the United States and Canada. There is also a very large community of **Black Muslims** in the United States. This community was established in the sixties in the heyday of Malcolm X (Abdul Malik Shabbazz) by Elijah Muhammad as **the Nation of Islam**. In the eighties, most Black Muslim groups accepted orthodox Islam and were proclaimed as an integral part of the ummah.

Malcom X was totally transformed when he went on a pilgrimage to Makkah.

I REALIZED THAT IF ALL THE DIFFERENT RACES SNORE IN THE SAME LANGUAGE, THEY MUST ALL BE EQUAL BEFORE GOD!

Organization of Islamic Conference

M uslim countries come together as a single international bloc at the Organization of Islamic Conference (OIC). The Organization was set set up at the initiative of King Faisal of Saudi Arabia in September 1969. Faisal called a summit of heads of state of Muslim countries as a result of the incident of arson at the al-Aqsa mosque in Jerusalem that year. The Summit established a permanent secretariat in Jeddah to coordinate activities of Muslim countries.

The Organization has three principle organs:

➭➭**1** The Islamic Summit of the Heads of the Muslim States which meets every three years to discuss major issues facing the Muslim world;

➭➭**2** the Conference of Foreign Ministers which meets yearly to implement general policy and review progress on resolutions; and

➭➭**3** the General Secretariat which promotes cooperation and coordinates activities between Muslim countries.

IS IT DOING ANYTHING WORTHWHILE?

Numerous institutions function under the umbrella of OIC, including: the Islamic Development Bank which finances projects throughout the Muslim world, the Red Crescent, the Islamic Science Foundation, the Islamic Centre for Development and Trade and Islamic Relief Agency.

The OIC has developed joint Muslim stands on a number of political issues, such as support for the people of Palestine, oppressed Muslim minorities as well as a number of Third World movements and issues. It has had some success in promoting economic and cultural cooperation between Muslim states and settling disputes between Muslim countries.

فلسطين
PALESTINE

The Iranian Revolution

I n its early phase, the Iranian revolution was a major source of inspiration for Muslims everywhere. It was considered the first serious victory of the traditionalists over the Westernized élites who were the main beneficiaries of the departing colonial powers. However, the revolution's excesses and injustices have turned most Muslims against it.

Yet justice, mercy and compassion are a cornerstone of the thought of the revolution's foremost intellectual, Ali Shariati (d. 1977). Shariati combined radical thought with socially conscious traditionalism. He was killed by the Shah and his works are banned in Iran. But his ideas continue to inspire Muslims everywhere.

The Iranian 'Islamic state' is uniquely Shia. The foremost authority is the **Wali Faqih** or the ruling jurist. In him resides all religious, political and legal authority: he is thus an absolute ruler. The **Wali Faqih** is assisted by a Revolutionary Council made up of the country's top religious authorities who are committed to the objectives of the revolution. Ayatollah Khomeini assumed the role of **Wali Faqih** after the revolution. His book **The Wilayat-e-Faqih** (Rule of the Theologian) sought to establish the legitimacy of the office.

There is also an elected parliament (**majlis**) which is controlled by a Speaker who is a leading member of the Shia clergy. Both the president (head of state) and the prime minister (head of government) are subordinates to the Wali Faqih.

Iran thus functions as an absolute theocracy. Sunni scholars have unanimously rejected theocracy as a form of Islamic government. The Iranian 'model' therefore cannot be exported to other Muslim countries.

Islamic Fundamentalism

In one respect, all Muslims are fundamentalists as they believe the Qur'an to be the literal Word of God. As such, the tendency to label anyone who speaks for Islam as 'fundamentalist' is not just meaningless, it is also dangerously wrong. The Muslims are not a monolithic entity. They include people with all shades of political opinions, positions and interpretations of Islam.

However, the last decades have seen a rise in fanaticism and intolerance amongst certain types of traditional Muslims. This highly visible and vocal group can be described as 'fundamentalist' in that it insists on a single interpretation of Islam which can only be manifested in terms of an 'Islamic state'. In this framework, the integrated, holistic and God-centred worldview of Islam is transformed into a totalitarian, theocratic world order and a persuasive moral God is replaced by a coercive, political one.

THE FUNDAMENTALISTS ARE ANGRY, ANTI MODERN AND AGGRESSIVELY ANTI-WEST. AND THEY HAVE VERY GOOD REASONS ON ALL COUNTS.

'Islam is the answer'. 'The Qur'an is our constitution'. Empty slogans reflect the total bankruptcy of fundamentalist thought.

157

Fundamentalism has emerged for a number of reasons:

⚙ **1.** The excesses of modernist leaders who have maintained their power in Muslim societies largely by coercive means and have ruthlessly persecuted the traditional leadership, including imprisonment, torture and execution of religious leaders and thinkers.

⚙ **2.** The spectacular failure of the economic and development policies of the modernist leaders which have led to the accumulation of wealth in fewer and fewer hands.

⚙ **3.** The continuous abuse and ridicule since the 50s of traditional thought, lifestyle and everything associated with it.

⚙ **4.** The policies of Western powers to deliberately undermine Islamic oppositions in Muslim countries, demonize Islamic leaders, prop up oppressive westernised regimes, and reduce Muslim states to economic paupers and debt-ridden societies.

THE MODERNISTS AND SECULARISTS HAVE A LOT TO ANSWER FOR.

The Islamic state

ince independence, Islamic movements all over the Muslim world have been working for the creation of an Islamic state in their respective countries. By an Islamic state is meant a state where the **Shariah**, or 'Islamic law', is established and the religious scholars, or the leaders of the national Islamic movement, either have some say in the government or have total control of political power.

❯ In recent times, a number of Muslim countries declared themselves to be Islamic states and ostensibly established the Shariah. But what is actually put into practice is a small number of classical juristic rulings concerning punishments, status of women and other spectacular aspects of classical jurisprudence. Thus, great show is made of 'Islamic punishments' or huddud laws, and floggings and amputations are advertised. These are in fact 'outer limit' laws to be carried out only under extreme conditions and after certain basic requirements of social justice, distribution of wealth, responsibilities of the state towards its citizens, mercy and compassion are fulfilled. What we thus get is an austere state operating on the basis of obscurantist and extremist law, behaving totally contrary to the teachings of the Qur'an and spirit of Islam, yet justifying its oppressions in the name of Islam! The self-declared Islamic states are thus nothing more than cynical instruments to justify the rule of a particular class, family or the military.

Women

raditional Muslim thought has been very unkind and oppressive to women. While religious scholars constantly recite the list of women's rights in Islam, they have been systematically undermining these very rights for centuries. While the Qur'anic injunctions are always directed towards 'the believing men' and 'the believing women', their interpretations conveniently forget the men and place all the burden on women.

For example, the Qur'anic advice about modesty in behaviour, 'tell the believing men to lower their gaze and to be mindful of their chastity...and tell the believing women to lower their gaze and to be mindful of their chastity...' (24: 30-31), has been interpretated exclusively in terms of the behaviour of women. 'Modest' and 'decent' behaviour for women in public has been interpreted as a rigid dress code despite the openness and much wider significance of the Qur'anic verses and their deliberate vagueness which are meant to allow all the time-bound changes that are necessary for social and moral growth of a society. In a total perversion of the Qur'anic advice, dressing modestly has thus been interpreted to mean dressing like a nun, covered from head to foot, showing only a woman's face (in some circles only the eyes), wrists and feet. An injunction meant to liberate from the oppressions of 'beauty' and 'fashion' ends as an instrument of oppression.

Over 1500 years ago Islam granted us the rights to own property, choose our own partners, divorce, abortion when necessary, education and sexual satisfaction in marriage.

But the list does not stop here...

Inverted and gender-biased interpretations of the teachings of the Qur'an and the Prophet Muhammad have led to a canonized jurisprudence which is aggressively anti-women. For example, while Islam insists that women have the right to divorce, Islamic jurisprudence has been formulated in such a way that it all but takes away this right. Judicial sleights of hands have been used throughout Muslim history to deny women a part in decision making, in playing their full part in society and generally to produce a thoroughly misogynist culture.

In some Muslim societies, women are doubly oppressed by grievous ethnic customs which are often justified in terms of Islam. While Islam explicitly forbids female circumcision, this brutality is maintained in the Sudan and Egypt in the name of religion. While Islam insists that women must choose their own partners, forced marriage is a common practice amongst the Muslims in India, Pakistan and Bangladesh.

The Prophet was asked:
Who should you honour
and befriend most?
He replied:
'Your mother,
then your mother,
then your mother,
then your father'.

The original teachings of Islam undermine patriarchy and replace it with a religious bond within which everyone – male or female, black or white, young or old, rich or poor – is equal. Islam aims at replacing 'paternal bond,' tribal allegiances and class affiliations, with allegiances based solely on moral and religious principles and total equality. But traditional thought and jurisprudence, as it has evolved, has undermined this goal as well as institutionalized injustices against women in the name of Islam.

Muslim women scholars have now begun to question the gender-biased interpretations of the Qur'an, the traditions of the Prophet and the early history of Islam. Writers like Azizah al-Hibri, Amina Wadud-Muhsin, Fatima Mernissi, Riffat Hassan, Laila Ahmad, Aisha Abdul-Rahman, Merryl Wyn Davies and so many others, who have more than just a passing familiarity with the classical sources, are set to introduce genuine equality in Muslim thought and action.

SURELY, THIS CAN'T BE RIGHT!

Reconstruction

I t had been customary for Muslim thinkers to blame the present condition of Muslim societies solely on colonialism. But in the 50s and 60s, the Algerian social philosopher Malek Bennabi (d.1973), knocked this suggestion for six. Bennabi introduced the theory of 'colonizability.' In essence, the theory holds that the real ills of the Muslim world do not spring from the fact of being colonized, but from a state previous to this, which made it ripe for colonization. The real liberation of Muslim people, Bennabi argued, will come from addressing the injustices introduced in the thought and body-politic of Islam in the late 13th century. Bennabi forced Muslim society to look at itself and re-examine its history and sources.

Other writers have offered similar analyses of the Muslim predicament. The Pakistani scholar, Fazlur Rahman (d.1988), consistently argued for re-examination of the formative history of Islam, a fresh understanding of the Qur'an from an ethical and systematic rather than atomistic perspective, and the growth of genuine, original and contemporary Islamic thought. Rahman's assertion that the development of Islamic law was not consistent with the ethical outlook of the Qur'an earned him as many friends as enemies.

The overall consensus amongst Muslim scholars is that the Muslim world is in urgent need of new thought which:

✏ **1**. Liberates tradition from fossilized history and transforms it from a suffocating into a life-enhancing enterprise.

✏ **2**. Formulates a new **fiqh** – that is, a new jurisprudence and law, focussed on contemporary needs, requirements and issues facing Muslim society.

✏ **3**. Re-opens 'the gates of **ijtihad**' and leads, through reasoned and sustained struggle, to a fresh understanding and a new comprehension of the teachings of the Qur'an and the life and traditions of the Prophet Muhammad.

I AGREE.

Islamization of knowledge

T he Palestinian thinker, Ismail al-Faruqi (d.1986), turned the quest for new thought into an international movement. He captured the imagination of Muslim intellectuals everywhere with his plans for the **Islamization of knowledge**. Al-Faruqi argued that Muslims were trying to solve their current and historic problems with tools, categories, concepts and modes of analysis that were not just irrelevant to their situation but, in many cases, inimical to the ethical spirit of Islam. The 'malaise of the ummah', al-Faruqi asserted, can only be treated by working on a systematic plan, to be carried out over a number of generations, that synthesized the best of classical Islamic knowledge and ideas with the best of contemporary thought. Only when modern knowledge has been 'Islamized' in this way, imbibed with the spirit and ethics of Islam, could it become an instrument for the mental and economic liberation of Muslim societies.

ISLĀMIZATION OF KNOWLEDGE:

GENERAL PRINCIPLES AND WORKPLAN

Isma'il Raji al Fārūqi

International Institute of Islām
1402/1982

While al-Faruqi's theories have been extensively criticized, not least for being too mechanical, his work unleashed tremendous pent up energy amongst Muslim intellectuals, academics, professionals, writers, journalists and thinkers. The Islamization of knowledge debate has now become central to any discussion of the nature of Muslim identity, the impact of modernity on Muslim society and ways of thinking about the present and future Muslim reality. The movement has generated vast amounts of innovative literature and induced a process of rethinking right across the Muslim world.

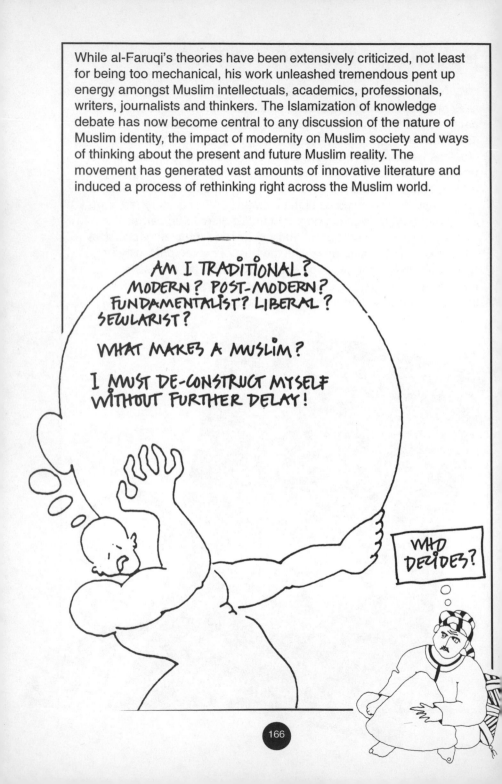

This rethinking has generated a number of new debates and disciplines. Islamic economics, for example, has emerged in the last two decades as a sophisticated discipline with its own categories, concepts, analytical tools and institutions. Operating on the basis of zero interest and participatory arrangements in the labour-capital and land-labour relationships, it addresses the questions of social welfare, unemployment, economic development, public debt and issues of global economic structure from the perspective of Islamic norms and values. Islamic banks have mushroomed all over the Muslim world.

→ A more recent and less conclusive debate concerns 'Islamic science'. Here the focus is on discovering a style of doing science that reflects the ethical teachings of Islam. Similar debates are raging about 'Islamic anthropology', 'Islamic sociology' and other social sciences. A number of new Islamic universities have been established to research and teach the emerging disciplines.

AGENDA
ISLAMIC SCIENCE
ISLAMIC ECONOMICS
ISLAMIC ARTS
ISLAMIC SOCIOLOGY
ISLAMIC ANTHROPOLOGY
AND ON AND ON . . .

Today and...

Barbaric. Bloodthirsty. Terrorists. Fundamentalists. Fanatics. Autocratic. Chauvinists. Sexists. Depraved. Medieval. Underdeveloped. Traditional.

These are just some of the terms that are constantly used to describe the followers of Prophet Muhammad. Such terms, and the images they portray, have a long history, a history going further back than the Crusades, of which the Rushdie affair is only the most recent episode. They defame and misrepresent over a billion people - one in four of all those who inhabit the planet earth - their societies, their histories, as caricatures of the darker side of the West.

But Muslims do not see themselves in this way.

I JOLLY WELL HOPE NOT!

Muslims are real people with real histories. For over eight hundred years their civilization led the world in science and learning, in thought and innovation, in literature and travel, in politics and international relations.

Today, Muslims are trying to rediscover their historic identity, liberate themselves from the crushing burdens of neo-colonialism and an oppressive and unjust world order, and shape a responsible and viable future.

...Tomorrow

B ehind the turmoil and contradictions which are pulling it in so many different directions, the Muslim world is reconstructing itself as a dynamic, progressive civilization of the future. Away from the clamour and slogans of a highly visible minority of extremists, it is bubbling with ideas, debates, and discussions on contemporary and future significance of the message of Muhammad. Many of these new ideas, theories, institutions and outlooks will not only transform Islam and Muslim societies from within, but will also make a genuine and original contribution to the evolution of a pluralistic world.

To be sure, the questions facing the Muslim world have neither simple answers nor are its problems amenable to palliative solutions. Sometimes the situation looks truly awesome and hopeless. But Muslims, by virtue of their faith, are eternal optimists. And they are becoming increasing aware that only sustained and prolonged intellectual, social and political effort, combined with a continuous process of rethinking, will yield viable options and alternatives for the future. Awareness, as they say, is half the battle!

Now that we have reached the end, here is a little secret. Many artists and photographers, Muslim and non-Muslim, past and present, have contributed to the mélange that is this book. I am sure they will appreciate that it is all for a good cause. We have run out of pages to mention all of them by name.

Was Salamu alaykum: peace be upon you and may your socks always keep you warm.

HEALTH WARNING

Although I have tried my best to keep the authors on a tightrope, I am sure that some of our brothers and sisters will find something to complain and whinge about. All complaints to the Speakers' Corner – please!

THE AUTHORS

Ziauddin Sardar is a writer, critic and broadcaster living in London. He has worked for the science journals *Nature* and *New Scientist* and London Weekend Television. Author of over thirty books on contemporary Islamic thought, science and technology in the Muslim world, information science and the future, he has contributed to numerous newspapers and magazines both in Britain and other parts of the world. Currently, he is editor of *Futures* and contributes regularly to the *New Statesman*.

Zafar Abbas Malik is a graphic designer living in London. He has designed numerous books and journals both for British and overseas publishers. He runs his own design company, Umran Design, and is the art director of the quarterly journal, *Arts and The Islamic World*.

Further Reading

GENERAL

Abdul Wahid Hamid, *Islam the Natural Way* (MELS, London). The best contemporary introduction to Islam.

Abdur-Rahman Azzam, *The Eternal Message of Muhammad* (Quartet). Acquiring a classic status.

Khurshid Ahmad (Ed), *Islam: Its Meaning and Message* (Islamic Foundation, Leicester). Weighty and worthy articles by noted modern Muslim thinkers.

Suzanne Haneef, *What Everyone Should Know about Islam and Muslims* (Kazi Publications, Chicago). A popular, lively book.

THE QUR'AN AND LIFE OF PROPHET MUHAMMAD

Muhammad Asad, *The Message of the Qur'an* (Dar al-Andalus, Gibraltar). Undoubtedly the best English translation of the Qur'an with a very informative and enlightened commentary.

Arthur J. Arberry, *The Koran Interpreted* (Oxford). A beautiful, poetic translation.

Muhammad Marmaduke Pickthall, *The Meaning of the Qur'an* (various editions). Widely used.

Sahih al-Bukhari, translated by Muhammad Muhsin Khan (Hilal Yayinlari, Ankara). An awkward translation of the classic collection of the sayings of the Prophet Muhammad.

Sahih al-Muslim, translated by Abdul Hameed Siddiqui, (Kitab Bhavan, New Delhi). Ditto.

Martin Lings, *Muhammad: His Life Based on Earliest Sources* (Allen and Unwin, London). Considered to be the best biography of Muhammad.

Muhammad Husayn Haykal, *The Life of Muhammad* (American Islamic Trust, Indianapolis). Translation of a highly regarded Arabic original.

CULTURE AND CIVILIZATION

Marshall Hodgson, *The Venture of Islam* (University of Chicago Press). A magnificent three volume journey through the ups and downs of Muslim civilization.

Ismael R. al-Faruqi and Lois Lamya al-Faruqi, *The Cultural Atlas of Islam* (Macmillan). Comprehensive!

D. M. Dunlop, *Arab Civilization to AD 1500* (Longman). Simply brilliant!

Majir Fakhry, *A History of Islamic Philosophy* (Longman). A well known introduction to the depth and sophistication of Islamic philosophy.

Ahmad Y. al-Hassan and Donald R. Hill, *Islamic Technology: An Illustrated History* (Cambridge). Highly readable standard text.

Hourani, Albert, *Arabic Thought in the Liberal Age* (Oxford University Press) and *A History of the Arab People* (Faber). Scholarly, but accessible.

George Makdisi, *The Rise of Colleges: Institutions and Learning in Islam and the West* (Edinburgh University Press). Shows just how much was borrowed from Islam!

Johannes Pederson, *The Arabic Book* (Princeton University Press). They published more books in 12th century Baghdad then they do today in London. Pederson shows how it was done.

F. Rosenthal, *Knowledge Triumphant* (Brill, Leiden). Explores the central importance of knowledge in Muslim civilization.

ISLAM AND THE WEST

Norman Daniel, *Heroes and Saracens: A Re-interpretation of the Chansons de Geste; Islam and the West: The Making of An Image* and *Islam, Europe and Empire* (Edinburgh University Press) – sourcebooks for the history of the demonization of Islam.

R. W. Southern, *Western Views of Islam in the Middle Ages* (Harvard University Press). At par with Daniel.

Amin Maalouf, *The Crusades Through Arab Eyes* (Al Saqi, London). Who was barbarian and who civilized? Maalouf gives eyewitness accounts.

Edward Said, *Orientalism* (Routledge, London). Much more widely read analysis.

Rana Kabbani, *Europe's Myths of the Orient* (Macmillan). Very good on artists and painters.

Ziauddin Sardar and Merryl Wyn Davies, *Distorted Imagination* (Grey Seal, London). Expands and updates Said and brings in the Rushdie affair.

ISLAM TODAY

Merryl Wyn Davies (Ed), *Beyond Frontiers: Islam and Contemporary Needs* (Mansell). Examines practical Muslim options.

Muhammad Nijatullah Siddiqui, *Muslim Economic Thinking* (Islamic Foundation, Leicester). An award-winning survey.

Syed Nawab Haider Naqwi, *Ethics and Economics: An Islamic Synthesis* (Islamic Foundation, Leicester). Essential for those interested in Islamic economics.

Hamid Enyat, *Modern Islamic Political Thought* (Macmillan). A ground breaking survey.

Merryl Wyn Davies, *Knowing One Another: Shaping an Islamic Anthropology* (Mansell, London). A tour through Islamic anthropology debate.

Fatima Mernissi, *Women and Islam* (Blackwell). A powerful feminist reinterpretation of Muslim theology.

Leila Ahmed, *Women and Gender in Islam* (Yale University Press). Ditto.

THE FUTURE

Ismael al-Faruqi, *Islamization of Knowledge* (International Institute of Islamic Thought, Washington). The master document of Islamization debate.

Ziauddin Sardar, *The Future of Muslim Civilization* and *Islamic Futures: The Shape of Ideas to Come* (Mansell, London). The titles say it all!

Alija Ali Izetbegovic, *Islam Between East and West* (American Trust Publications, Indianapolis). An integrated analysis of the human condition from a noted scholar and President of Bosnia-Herzegovina.

M. Umar Chapra, *Islam and the Economic Challenge* (Islamic Foundation, Leicester). Brilliant analysis of Islamic economics as future alternative to capitalism.

Index and Little Dictionary